TRY BEING A TEENAGER

A CHALLENGE TO PARENTS TO STAY IN TOUCH

EARL D. WILSON

TRY BEING A TEENAGER

A CHALLENGE TO PARENTS TO STAY IN TOUCH

MULTNOMAH · PRESS

Portland, Oregon 97266

Unless otherwise identified, all Scripture references are from the *Holy Bible: New International Version,* copyright 1978 by the New York International Bible Society. Used by permission of Zondervan Bible Publishers.

Cover Design by Britt Taylor Collins
Text Design by Donna Johnson

© 1982 by Multnomah Press
Printed in the United States of America

Library of Congress Cataloging in Publication Data

Wilson, Earl D., 1939-
   You try being a teenager!

   Includes bibliographical references.
      1. Parenting—Religious aspects—Christianity.
2. Parent and child.   3. Adolescent psychology.
4. Conflict of generations.   5. Interpersonal communication.
I. Title.
HQ755.8.W54   1982   649'.125   82-8314
ISBN 0-930014-97-9 (pbk.)

              86   87   88   89   90   –   11   10   9   8   7   6   5   4   3

I affectionately dedicate this book to five very special people, our children—Marcy, Mark, Mike, Melissa, and Michelle. They have shared their lives with Sandy and me, and through the book they are sharing their lives with you, the reader. They are teaching us that living with teenagers is fun.

Thank you, Marcy.
Thank you, Mark.
Thank you, Mike.
Thank you, Melissa.
Thank you, Michelle.

You are special and we love each of you very much.

Your Dad.

Table of Contents

Introduction

As a parent I have become increasingly aware of how little we understand the process of helping our children move from childhood to adulthood. As a counselor of adolescents and their parents, I am amazed that such beautiful people sometimes act so ugly toward each other. Why? The answer is often because they just don't understand each other. My wife, Sandy, and I have dedicated ourselves to trying to understand both parents and teenagers. This book reflects some of the things we have learned. It is *our* book, although I have done the labor of putting our insights on paper and thus bear full responsibility for the final product.

I am convinced that during the adolescent period, parents must focus on one primary task. That task is *not* correcting, controlling, or even training. The task is *staying in touch.* By the time the young person reaches age twelve or thirteen, most of the training and corrective functions have been completed. We must now become consultants and guides instead of directors. This does not mean that we give up our God-given authority and responsibility. It only means that we deliberately choose to discharge that responsibility in some new ways. To love at this point is to stay in contact while letting go. It is only as we do this that we are able to see how well we have done. What makes this process difficult, however, is trying to learn an entirely new set of rules. It is my prayer that the pages which follow will help you understand teenagers in general and your teenager in particular.

This book is written because one of my students, Glenda Loomis, took a course in Adolescent Psychology from me, and felt that some of the insights God was giving Sandy and me should be shared with others. Glenda backed up her conviction by being willing to help me with some of the technical aspects of the writing. For this I am extremely grateful. I also wish to acknowledge the contribution of my secretary, Kay Quick, who typed the rough draft of the manuscript and served as a constant source of encouragement during the process of preparing the manuscript.

Earl D. Wilson, Ph.D.

Chapter 1

Living with Your Teen: Joy or Trial by Fire?

Jesus loved the little children, but He didn't have to live with my teenagers.

For many people, being the parent of a teenager is a fearful thing. It isn't easy! A frantic parent put it bluntly: "You ought to bury them at twelve and dig them up at eighteen." That captures the sentiments of many parents today.

Freudian psychology has brainwashed us into believing that the only possible positive impact we have on our child is during the first seven years of his or her life. This is not only untrue, but it also sets us up for extreme feelings of failure and hopelessness when our adolescents begin to become people in their own right. Our fears of the teenage years are maintained by our failure to understand the developmental process by which children are transformed into autonomous adults. Our problems are further compounded by the fact that the skills which we as parents found helpful during our children's early years now suddenly seem obsolete. Facing such a heavy responsibility as parenting teens while feeling totally unprepared for the task is frightening. One parent said, "I don't even know *what* to do with my teenager, let alone *how* to do it."

A relatively successful mother consulted her pastor because she was seriously distressed over the way things were going with her children. The pastor, searching desperately for some words of comfort, reminded this mother how Jesus loved children. Her reply was to the point: "Jesus loved the little children all right, but He didn't have to live with my teenagers!" Statements such as this reflect the sentiment of many that raising teenagers is a trial by fire.

11

The famous American psychologist Dr. G. Stanley Hall referred to adolescence as the period of storm and stress. Any parent knows this. What parents do not seem to know is *why* adolescence is a period of storm and stress or *what* to do about it.

Many Christian parents who place a heavy emphasis upon trying to *"train a child in the way he should go"* (Proverbs 22:6) feel totally frustrated during their child's teenage years. One parent said, "I hardly feel like a Christian when all of these things are happening with my child." Another said, "If this is God's plan for me, He must have a weird sense of humor."

Discovering the Joy of Parenting Teens

As the father of five children and a frequent counselor of adolescents, I often wondered, "What is parenting teenagers going to be like for us?" I felt my children were caught in a fishbowl. They not only had to struggle with the normal tasks that go with growing up, but they had a "shrink" for a father. My wife, Sandy, and I labored under the burden of trying to raise godly children while maintaining a good image as a professional family. We were putting tremendous pressure on ourselves, and this was being transmitted to our children as they approached the teen years.

Fortunately, God put us in contact with a couple who could help us. I was speaking at the time for a family conference at Bear Trap Ranch in Colorado. We met a Christian physician and his wife there who were excited about the good times they were having with their four children. "The teen years are the great years," they said. "These are the years of greatest joy. Seeing what God is doing in the lives of our teenagers is so much fun. They are becoming real people, and we can talk to them."

Sandy and I pondered these statements frequently after we first met Berne and Jaci. We made a conscious effort to model our attitudes after theirs and to begin to look at the job of parenting teens as a joy instead of a trial by fire. We are now in the middle of that process. Counting John, our American Field Service exchange student from Ghana, we have four teenagers. Last evening there were ten children at our table and eight of them were teens. As Sandy and I retreated from the dining room following dinner and found some quiet moments in our room, we were impressed with the beauty of God manifested through those ten people.

If this book accomplishes nothing else, our hope is that you will be led to see your teens as special. This will be easier to do as you grasp a better understanding of their psychological development and learn how to relate to them better.

Barriers to Good Parent-Teen Relationships

As I talk to my own teenagers and to the many teenagers I have opportunity to counsel, I discover that parents and teens usually want the same thing. They want to relate to each other and to be able to enjoy each other. Clearly, this does not always happen. In fact, relating to and enjoying each other may be the exception rather than the rule. One sixteen-year-old boy said, "There seems to be a wall between my parents and me. We used to be able to talk, but not now." If the teen years are going to be years of joy rather than trial, being able to understand some of the barriers which get in the way is important.

Barrier #1: Lack of Communication

Lack of communication is a common barrier between parents and their teens. Parents report that they try to communicate but nothing happens. Teens say, "I just wish they would talk to me once without yelling." Many homes are stalemated. A father said sadly, "We just don't seem to speak the same language." Communication difficulties develop between parent and teen because we labor under the misconception that if two people want to communicate, they will know how to communicate. We should know better because we experience communication difficulties with our friends and spouses, as well as with our teens. Successful communication is a skill and needs to be developed just as learning to cook, playing golf, or solving a Rubik's cube. It doesn't come naturally. Chapter 6 discusses the communication barrier in detail and focuses upon some skill development tasks which will make you and your teen more successful in communicating with each other.

Barrier #2: Power Struggles

When communication skills are not present, we slide into the belief that the problem is caused by the other person not wanting to talk. "He just doesn't care," is offered as an analysis of the problem. This belief results in another major barrier, the power struggle. One of the important tasks of the developing adolescent is achieving a sense of autonomy (see chapter 9), which is best accomplished by thinking one's own thoughts. This does not mean that the teenager does not want to discuss those thoughts. But he does not want those thoughts taken away from him.

When parents push for more talk, without understanding the need for the adolescent to set the pace, a power struggle develops. Only bad things happen when the parent is trying to get into the youngster's thoughts, because the child will keep the door closed even though he longs to know what the parent thinks. The key is to be available without being obtrusive.

I remember working with our son, Mark. As we put shingles on the garage roof he told me something was bothering him. In true counselor fashion I said, "Would you like to tell me about it?" "No," he replied. I was shocked. "This is terrible," I thought. "Doesn't he know I could help him solve the problem?" Several times that afternoon I tried to go back and pry open the door. Each time he made it clear that he didn't want me inside. How frustrating! Fortunately I gave up when I realized he was beginning to pull back from me.

The next day I said, "Did you get that problem worked out?" "Oh yeah, thanks," he said. But he never told me what it was. I have to assume that what took place in his private thoughts was what he needed. Otherwise I run the risk of creating a power struggle, which destroys the opportunity to share his thoughts at a later time when I am needed. I relax when I remind myself that he is a level-headed person and is capable of making pretty good decisions.

Barrier #3: Value Conflicts

A third barrier results from a conflict in values. By the time you are a parent, you feel you have earned the right to be dogmatic. There is one major problem. *You are not always right.* (This is okay for me to write. Your teenagers know it already anyway.) Dogmatism results in an inability to separate facts from opinions. Teenagers are usually better educated than their parents, and they draw their own conclusions and make their own distinctions between truth and opinion. (*They* are not always right either—but I guess I don't need to tell you that.) Different perceptions and different interpretations result in conflict and the construction of barriers second only to the barriers created by a power struggle.

It is important for the adolescent to sort and select values and ideals by which he will run his life. As a parent, I have a strong vested interest in the teen selecting my ideals and values or a set which is close to mine. Often I demand that my values be accepted without giving my children the opportunity to try them on for size and reject them if they don't fit. My goal should be to be available to them as a resource while they do the work for themselves. This idea is elaborated in chapter 8. The harder I press my teens to accept my values, the greater the possibility will be that they will reject them. I need to spell out my values in such a way that they will be understood by my teenagers, but I must also place a high priority upon hearing and accepting their views.

If you are worried about this area, be encouraged to know that teenagers often defend family values to others at the same time they are challenging them within the family context. This is an important part of developing a personal value system. Don't thwart it. Thwarting this and other processes of personal growth is probably one of the problems which the Apostle Paul had in mind when he warned: *"Fathers, do not exasperate your children; instead, bring them up in the training and instruction of the Lord"* (Ephesians 6:4).

Barrier #4: Lack of Time Together

A fourth barrier to good parent-teen relationships is lack of time involvement. The barriers are interrelated. If you want your teen to talk, spend time with him. Unhurried time. Teenagers get sick and tired of being rushed. I believe spending time with children during the teen years is more important than at any other time. Unfortunately, we often smother children as preschoolers and starve them during the teen years.

Each year during our private vacation, Sandy and I discuss what we believe to be the needs of each of our children. (You need a private vacation when you have five children.) One year we decided that we would try to make ourselves more available to our children, particularly the older ones. We have been amazed at the benefits. They talk, they laugh, they play, sometimes they sulk or cry, but the fact is they enjoy and need the time together with us.

Do not try to schedule time together or try to compete with their friends. It won't work. Simply discover when they have time to kill. That's when they need you and will love to be with you. If you are always rushing or trying to regiment their lives, they will withdraw. Be there when they get home from school. Be there when they return from the ball game. Be there when they win and be there when they lose.

I often hear parents say, "It's quality, not quantity, that counts." This is not true. You will not have quality without quantity. Building relationships with adolescents is like developing a good sex life—it takes time. We have found that the best times are the relaxed times when we interact one-to-one with a child, doing something he is interested in doing. Group time is important, but it is no substitute for personal time. When you and your teenager are relaxed and enjoying each other, good conversations result. During these times, if you ask them what they think about something, you will get an honest answer. You will be amazed when they ask you what *you* think, and occasionally they will even ask for your advice. Savor the opportunity.

Think how degrading it is to be told that your parents are too busy to spend time with you. Teenagers are smart enough to know that busyness is a choice. If you are too busy to spend time with them, they know inside that you are choosing other things ahead of them. Think about it.

Don't get discouraged if you ask them to spend time and they turn you down. They will say "Yes" when they need the time. Just by asking you have gone up ten points on their scale. Time is money, but time is also the substance from which good relationships are built.

Barrier #5: Linking Personal Worth to Performance

Another barrier to relationship building is allowing your worth as a parent to be tied up in the performance of the child. This barrier is erected in one of two ways. One way is in living out your life through the accomplishments of the child.

As a frustrated athlete I find it easy to seek acceptance for myself through the athletic accomplishments of my children. Each time Marcy scores an ace in volleyball I feel as though I have accomplished something. I feel like I am the participant in each race that Mike runs or each match he wrestles. The problems with this are obvious. What about the serves that go out of bounds? What about the races or wrestling matches that are lost? How can I expect my children to learn to accept their defeats, as well as their victories, if I have trouble accepting their losses?

My thirteen-year-old son, Mike, and I have discussed this on several occasions. I have asked his forgiveness for the pressure I put on him at times. He has identified those times when I need to back off and has told me to do so. He now knows that I want him to do his best for himself rather than just for me. I was in danger of erecting an enormous barrier until I decided to focus on his needs rather than my inappropriate ones.

The second way this barrier is erected is by tying your worth (or lack of worth) to the unacceptable behavior of your child. You may be a good Christian even if your children do things that you would never do. Although it is true that God holds us responsible for the way we raise our children, it is not true that if we do everything right they will turn out right. There is even some question from historians as to whether or not the half brothers and sisters of Jesus turned out right. After the death of Joseph, Jesus was apparently the man of the house and therefore was responsible for rearing His younger siblings. Though Jesus never did anything wrong, many things He did were seen as failures by His contemporaries, including raising His siblings.[1] Because God allows people to make individual choices, we can raise our children almost perfectly and yet see results which are less than what we wish to see.

We must also remember that God is sovereign and will continue to work in the lives of our children even after they are no longer at home. As a parent, I take comfort in applying the words of Philippians 1:6 to my children as well as to myself: *"Being confident of this, that he who began a good work in you will carry it on to completion until the day of Christ Jesus."*

Barrier #6: *Monopolizing Decision Making*

Not allowing teenagers to make decisions for themselves is another barrier to relationship building. When our children are young, we make most of their decisions for them. We tell them when to get up and when to go to bed. We tell them what to wear and when to wear it. We tell them who to play with and how they may play. If we are not careful, we will raise children who are ready to go to college, but who are not able to make the decisions college life requires.

Our responsibility as parents is to train our children to make decisions. We do this by providing examples of decision making, and by providing opportunities for them to practice making decisions themselves. Some of these decisions are small—such as letting a child decide to wear a dress or jeans. However significant the decision is, when the choice is made, we get to know our child better by observing his preferences and the influences which affect those preferences.

When we allow our child to make choices, we also help him know how to stand up against pressures that he doesn't like, such as the teasing of other children, or demands that he dress or act in a certain way. I believe that young people need to be helped to decide what kind of friends they wish to have. If this is done with sensitivity and compassion, the power struggle over friends will be avoided. This is a touchy area because our child's friends and their families may not share our values. The key is to avoid being panicked by this, and to try to help the youngster evaluate the basis for deciding about friends.

One of our children formed a strong friendship with a neighbor and began to spend a lot of time with him. Soon after the friendship began to develop, other people would say such things as, "Surely you don't let Mark play with Johnny!" This disturbed us greatly, but we did not have any information that would suggest breaking up the relationship. After some prayer and consideration, we decided to let Mark decide about whether or not to continue the relationship. We also hoped to teach him how to decide about matters of this importance. We called him in and told him what we had heard. At first he became defensive and I could see him begin to pull away from us. A barrier was beginning to form. "Wait!" I said. "We are not saying you can't play with Johnny." He became less tense and began to listen. "We only want you to know these things so you can decide whether or not he is a good friend to you. The things we have been told may not even be true."

Mark agreed to keep his eyes open and to talk with us periodically about what he felt was going on. He further agreed to come home if he saw things he felt he should not be involved in. In two years he has come home on this basis a time or two. All the data is not in. Only time will tell how good a decision this was on our part. One thing is certain—giving Mark the decision and having confidence in him has kept down the barrier, and has helped us develop greater confidence in his ability to make good decisions in the future. He also feels closer to us because he feels that we respect him as a person with a brain. I might add that when the boys were younger we decided not to let them play with the older neighbor boys since we felt they could not handle that type of pressure. That, too, was a good decision.

Our teenagers often ask, "Why didn't you let me know?" or "Why didn't you ask me?" Both of these statements reveal the desire that adolescents have to be included in decisions. They don't like surprises and we, as parents, need to respect that part of them. Information is essential to the decision making process. We need to share relevant information with our adolescents if we expect them to make wise decisions.

Sandy and I have tried to establish a pattern for decision making in our family. Some decisions are for us as parents to make, other decisions are for our teens to make, and some decisions we need to make jointly.

Adolescents are much more apt to accept that rank has its privilege if they feel that you respect them enough to give them some decisions to make. Teenagers don't need to make all of the mistakes in the world in order to become good decision makers, but having an opportunity to make a few of the less harmful mistakes may be helpful. Teaching your teens to make decisions will avoid creating a barrier and will make your relationship much stronger because of the mutual respect which is generated.

The Opportunities of Adolescence

The adolescent years are not only tolerable as barriers are overcome, but are in fact years full of opportunities for you and your children. The opportunity for *friendships as equals* rather than as a superior to an inferior is very important, for example. This gangly, beautiful person in your house no longer needs to be treated as weak, but can be accepted as strong, competent, insightful, and intelligent. What a joy to be out from under the burden of caring for someone weaker. How much better to develop a give-and-take relationship with an equal who is like you, but who is also a person in his own right.

A second opportunity is the chance for *intellectual companionship.* As my friend Berne has said, "It is great to talk to them as equals. They have ideas, and many of them are good." Let your adolescents try out their ideas. Pick their brains. Find out just how bright they really are. You will be pleasantly surprised to find out that they know more about the economy or modern ballet than you do, perhaps. They will share their lives with you if you acknowledge how intelligent they really are.

Adolescence is a second chance. Freudian psychology places heavy emphasis upon the first seven years of a child's life. I believe, however, that ages eleven to eighteen are an even greater opportunity because, as the child's capacity for abstract thinking develops, they begin to re-work much of their earlier development. This new ability to think often results in significant changes in personality. Peter said, "I'm amazed at me! I'm a new person! Even Dad says I've got a pretty good head on my shoulders." Abstract thinking allows us to discuss values, ideals, and moral issues, and to better understand our differences. This tremendous opportunity will be discussed in more detail in chapters 7 and 8.

Another opportunity is the opportunity to *work yourself out of a job.* We need to realize that parenting is not our only role in life. When the job is finished, we can concentrate our efforts on other enjoyable pursuits. Many parents who come to me for consultation have finished their work and have done a good job, only they don't know it. Our job is to do the rough carpentry work. God is the finish carpenter. The teen years are years in which we can wisely let go. My friend Paul Welter has clearly stated just how important this step is.

If you have been worrying about whether your children will turn out all right, has your worrying helped? If you have been looking forward to the day when your children will match the ideal in your mind, has this kept you from enjoying them just like they are right now? A person who lives in the future is always anxious. As Christians we are concerned about the future. Yet Jesus, who taught so much about the future and made our own future possible, urged His followers to be aware of the present. "Don't be anxious about tomorrow," He taught. "Do not be anxious about your life" (a future-oriented activity) but rather, "Seek first His kingdom (meaning His rule) and His righteousness, and all these things shall be yours as well" (Matthew 6:33).[2]

I could elaborate other opportunities, but at this point I want to simply say that parenting teens can be a very pleasurable, although frightening, experience. Take the risk! Trust God to help you relax and live with your teens. The rest of this book will help you to develop an understanding of teens, and to develop the skills which are necessary to relate to your adolescent. The final chapters will provide practical help in dealing with some of the practical issues (such as conflicts) and special needs (such as developing self-esteem) that arise.

Footnotes

[1]To imply that Jesus "failed" to raise His younger siblings to be mature, godly men and women does not mean He committed a sin or was less than the perfect Son of God.
[2]Paul Welter, *Family Problems and Predicaments: How to Respond* (Wheaton, Ill.: Tyndale House, 1977), p. 241.

Chapter 2

Understanding Your Teen Psychologically

I don't understand this person, Lord.
What's going on?

In one of my weaker moments I decided that I would be much happier if there were more people like me. My professional credentials have given me an expectation that I should be able to understand others, and yet I am constantly amazed at how confusing people often are. On the other hand, I am painfully aware of those times when I feel totally misunderstood by others.

As I listen to adolescents and to their parents I realize that parent-teen relationships are *full* of misunderstandings. Parents become so involved in the task of raising their children that they lose contact with them as people. My son reminded me of this danger recently by saying, "You know, Dad, I'm not like you." As I processed his words, I said to myself, "If he is not like me, and I want to stay in touch with him, I better figure out what he is like."

In this chapter we will seek to discover what teenagers are like. The stages of development of a teenager from a dependent child to an autonomous adult are presented first. Then special attention is given to each area of growth. Understanding the psychological development of teenagers will help you to better understand and relate to your own teenager, and to adjust to the changes that are taking place in his or her life.

Stages of Growth and Development

At the risk of being simplistic, I define an adolescent as an adult trying to happen. In order for adulthood to take place, adolescents must escape the dependent state called childhood. This attempted escape sets up a serious conflict with parents who believe that their role is to keep the child in captivity. It is important to note that at the same time the adolescent is trying to escape the control of his parents, he is also trying to escape from the mind and body of the child. This is very frustrating both to the adolescent and to the parents.

When parents become frustrated with adolescent behavior they often ask, "Why do you do things like that?" The adolescent, who is just as frustrated, may respond by saying, "I don't know why! I just did it." This type of interchange often sets up a power struggle between a parent who needs to understand the adolescent, and an adolescent who needs to understand himself. Interestingly enough, both want the same things, but they end up miles apart in their search.

Many psychologists and educators have found it helpful to view human development in various stages that span our experiences from the cradle to the grave. The age boundaries for each of these stages are somewhat arbitrary. The key issue for our purposes is to identify what is happening to the person in each area of development: physical, social, intellectual, as well as moral and spiritual. The combined results of these areas in the development of a person results in what we call "personality." In Figure 1 I have listed five stages and have given examples of the development which takes place at each stage.

STAGES OF HUMAN DEVELOPMENT

	Physical	Social	Intellectual	Moral & Spiritual
Childhood 0–10	Constant non-dramatic growth. Slow development of coordination.	Focus on self and learning social skills. Identity school-oriented. Social dependence strong.	No view of objective reality. Motoric perception controls reason.	Egocentrism. Parroting of values. Easily influenced.
Pre-Adolescence 11–13	Sexual maturation and rapid physical growth begins. Coordination development increases.	Vascillation between periods of friendship and isolation. Social dependence continues.	Complete generality of thought. Spurts of abstraction. Concreteness of thought.	Other-awareness emerges. Parental values present. Legalistic black and white thinking.
Adolescence 14–20	Period of rapid growth and sexual maturation. Changes in voice and sex related characteristics.	Peer group focus. Weakened ties with family. Emerging social independence.	Ability to deal with hypothetical issues. Propositional thinking. Formal reasoning begins.	Development of strong idealism. Questioning of previous values. Spiritual inquisitiveness.
Adult 1 21–45	Physical stability. Full development achieved.	Upward mobility. Family development and family focus. Social independence.	Intellectual growth slows but continues with experience.	Move from idealism to realism. Spiritual lethargy.
Adult 2 46–N	Physical decline and aging.	Vocational decline. Family dispersement. Couple friendships. Social dependence emerging.	Intellectual decline, but productivity continues throughout healthy life.	Moral and spiritual entrenchment the rule. Spiritual unrest the exception.

Figure 1

The Adolescent and Physical Development

If there is anything obvious about teenagers, it is the fact that they are changing physically. They are growing outwardly and they are maturing inwardly. Loads that could not be carried by a ten-year-old are proudly hoisted by a teen with one hand. Change of voice is so obvious it becomes a source of embarrassment for either the teenager or his parents. Creamy cheeks become infected with pimples or covered with whiskers. These and other physical changes become a source for adolescent egocentrism. The body takes on new importance and thoughts about the body often preoccupy the teenager.

The changes that occur are not all muscle or bone. Hormonal changes are occurring as well. Almost overnight the sexually disinterested teenager becomes highly interested in the opposite sex. Physical appearance which was once neglected now becomes a priority. Some of these changes are cheerfully welcomed by parents. We think it's about time he learned to comb his hair. Other changes such as overt sexual interest cause us to be fearful. We wish that they were all grown up.

Physical development has three basic aspects we need to consider: (1) general physical growth, (2) sexual maturation, and (3) development of physical appearance and abilities. We will briefly examine each area and point out some of the important aspects of each type of growth.

General Physical Growth

If you have ever gone through the experience of not being recognized by a friend because of some changes which have occurred, you may be able to identify with your teenager during the general physical growth period. Physically many teenagers undergo dramatic changes within a very short period of time. Those who are growing rapidly struggle to adjust to their new body. Those who mature late grapple with feelings of inferiority. The overall result is turmoil. No one is the same, but everyone seems to be upset in one way or another. Jersild, Brook, and Brook make several important observations about this period of change.

> Physical changes have important psychological repercussions as youngsters adapt themselves to their changing bodies and to the surge in their sexual capacities. The boy, although still so young that it seems incongruous to picture him as a father, becomes a potential mate. The girl has the figure of a woman al-

though she is scarcely accustomed to her new clothes. It takes time for adolescents to get used to their new equipment and to adjust to changes in their body and proportions.[1]

What are the responsibilities of the parents while all these changes are taking place? Is there anything that the parent should do to help the teenager through this difficult time? Here are some suggestions for parents to use to make a healthy impact during this period.

1. *Emphasize the normal aspects of what is going on.* If your child is an early developer, help him to realize that he got there first and may be through growing by the time some others get started. Some adolescents who mature early fear that the growth process may never stop. They are not comforted by statements such as, "You will probably be a good basketball player." At that moment they probably feel too awkward to even walk. The later developer needs help in realizing that his time will come. Parents need to be careful not to criticize attempts by the youngster to speed up the process. Let them know that you realize that waiting is hard.

2. *Try to understand their feelings rather than telling them how to feel.* Empathy is much more important than telling them how it was for you. Remember your job is not to fix things for your teenager. You can't make them grow more or less, faster or stronger. You can't even make them feel better. They don't need to feel better. They need to feel understood.

3. *Encourage them to openly discuss their questions about their physique.* One day my wife became aware that our daughter Marcy (who is adopted) was in a very contemplative mood. She was growing rapidly and she was also seeking to adjust to her awareness that she is not our natural child. Sandy said to her, "I know what your mother looked like." Marcy's response was, "You do? Have you met her?" Sandy said, "She is beautiful." "How do you know?" Marcy asked. "Have you seen her?" Sandy responded by saying, "I haven't met her, but I am sure she is beautiful because I am sure she looks like you." Relationships are built in this type of openness, and the fears of teens are lessened.

4. *Don't force your teenager to be too practical during this tense period.* Many practical parents believe in getting every ounce of wear out of clothes. They also believe in buying clothes that will be outworn before they are outgrown. When adolescents are growing rapidly, they often do not wear out a pair of jeans before they outgrow them. This has caused many parents to insist that their teenagers buy cheaper jeans or wear hand-me-downs. When this happens, the teen-

ager feels not only strange but misunderstood and unloved. They feel bad to start with, and now their parents are forcing them to be unstylish. They feel like insult has been added to injury.

A similar thing may happen in the area of hairstyling. I am a person who enjoys trying to find the cheapest haircut in town. If there is a decent three dollar haircut around, I will find it. My children, on the other hand, want to be stylish. They seem to migrate to the most expensive shop. When this happens, my practical nature gets on a collision course with their need for physical acceptance and stylishness. I don't intend to injure them, but I do sometimes.

We have found some solutions which work for us. We allow a certain dollar amount for either jeans or haircuts. If the teenager wants the most expensive, we will not deny them that privilege, but will help them to determine how to earn the money to pay the difference. This has been a useful technique in teaching them the value of things and the relationship between work and reward. We have also tried to encourage them to wear hand-me-downs, but to do it secretly. They can choose to save their money and wear the older pants which are in style even if they were their older brother's pants. Once they have tried this and found that they are not ridiculed, they are usually quite cooperative. A wise parent will allow the teenager to have a say in the styles chosen because teenagers know more than their parents in this area.

The period of physical growth is at best a period of great tension for both parents and teenagers alike. It can be a period of relationship building, however, if parents are sensitive to the needs of the adolescent and offer emotional support during this period.

Sexual Maturation

The aspect of puberty introduces not only physical growth, but also the process of sexual maturation. What role can the parents play during this process? The most common response of parents to adolescents' physical maturation is to begin to caution or lecture them about the responsibilities that go along with sexuality. This is probably the *least* helpful thing that you can do, particularly if your teenager realizes that you have trouble accepting your own sexuality. Obviously the relationship between sexuality and responsibility needs to be taught, but not taught by threats or fear. Sexuality is a gift from God that needs to be accepted with joy and celebration, not fear and trepidation.

One of my colleagues has followed the practice of taking each of his daughters out to eat to celebrate their birthdays. He begins this practice when they turn eight years old. He points out to them how proud he is of them and how proud they should be to be a woman. These "dates" allow the girls to dress up and begin to learn some social graces. He has also used these dates as an occasion to let them ask questions about their sexuality and about the differences between men and women. This practice has served as a base for other discussions about sexual behavior, and has provided input into the sexual standards their girls are developing. Celebrations naturally spark discussion, while lectures signal the need for silence for most teenagers.

Teenagers today have an ample amount of information about sexuality. What they don't have is a framework for living out this aspect of their lives. This problem is compounded when parents are unwilling to share their attitudes and experiences with their children. One adolescent said, "I know that my parents do it but they act like they don't know I know. It would be so much easier if they would just talk to me." My oldest child has often said, "Dad, I may have virgin ears, but I'm not a child. I do know some things, you know." Most teenagers would love to be able to talk to their parents about sex, especially when there were no issues of conflict.

Unfortunately, parents usually wait until they want to correct some sexual misconduct before they are willing to discuss this area with their teenager. At that point, however, the teenager is in a defensive stance and is not very receptive to the parents' ideas. A consideration of the importance of making good choices related to sex is most helpful *before* bad choices have been made. Once a teenager has made a mistake he usually realizes his error and then needs support and guidance to a better way, not a rehearsal of the error.

In her helpful book, *What to Say After You Clear Your Throat,* Jean Gochros has a chapter entitled, "The Open Doors Policy." By opening doors, she means that parents must continually be providing an atmosphere in which open discussions about sex can take place. This policy should begin early in childhood and should continue as the youngster reaches adolescence.

When doors are open, be sensitive to the door and don't drive through it with a Mack truck. When my oldest son was about nine he called me to the family room with cries of, "Dad, come quick." I bounded up the stairs thinking someone was hurt. He stood pointing at the television, asking, "What is that? What are they doing?" Quickly I realized that he was watching a nature program about fish. The sequence on the screen was picturesquely presenting the reproductive process. The female had laid the eggs in a trench and the male was swimming over them, fertilizing them with a spray of sperm.

As I stood by him and verbally described what we were watching, I decided to take advantage of this moment for some further education. The door seemed to be open. When the sequence was finished I took a quick, deep breath and said, "You know, people aren't like fish. People are . . ." After three or four minutes of talk about sex for people, I felt very proud of myself and relieved enough to look down. He was gone! He wasn't even in the room. The only conclusion I could reach was that he knew all he needed to know at that moment about people. He just wanted to know about fish.

When your child becomes a teenager he needs and often wants to know more. Open doors with him and share attitudes and feelings as well as information. Share an attitude that sex is a good gift from God and that it is best when it is responsibly used as God intended. Be available to empathize with your teenager's fears and embarrassment as he makes mistakes or feels awkward because of where he is in the maturation process. Creating frequent "special" times for discussions facilitates this aspect of your relationship.

Development of Physical Appearance and Abilities

Teens are also strongly impacted by the development of their physical appearance and abilities. During adolescence the body is often the major source of acceptance for the teenager. If your body is strong and athletic you are accepted. If your body is petite and pretty you are also accepted. Admiration of the beauty of the body of the opposite sex is very common. In recent years it has even become much more acceptable for women to admire the male body. Some parents have difficulty handling these changes. Many adolescents suffer greatly because they are unable to find acceptance based on their looks or physical abilities. Parents need to be sensitive to the feelings of rejection their adolescents experience. They need to help them find other appropriate ways of gaining acceptance.

Friendliness, for example, is a valuable skill which parents neglect in training their children. Friendliness bridges the gap when acceptance based upon physical attractiveness alone is impossible. Learning new skills and new attitudes is a very important developmental task for all adolescents, especially for those whose physical development does not gain them immediate acceptance.

As a parent, I have found two important hurdles I must help my teenagers overcome. Both are related to physical appearance and abilities. The first is not making the team. This can be devastating for a teen and parents must be available to help their adolescent work it through. Don't tell them it isn't important. They will never believe you. Let them know that you know how important it is to them, and stay close as they regroup and try something new.

The second concern is not being asked for a date. This may be especially devastating for young ladies who have been culturally persuaded that if you aren't popular with the boys you have no value. Help them to focus on the kind of boys they like and what they would like to experience in a relationship. This may result in new hope.

Your attitudes as a parent toward your child's athletic or dating success are crucial. Are you placing too much value in these areas and thus putting additional pressure on your child? Don't add your rejection to that which they already feel from their peers. Live your own life. Don't expect your child to provide all the excitement for you.

Times of disappointment may also provide the parent with an opportunity to model coping skills. The adolescent will watch you closely to see if you have some ways of handling disappointment which he or she could use. They don't need to learn how to be a basket case. They need to see evidence that God is alive and well even when we experience disappointments. Show them a better way.

Physical development is important. It is important because it opens the door to new aspects of life and relationships. It is uncharted territory for the adolescent. As a parent you should seek to give direction and to be available to provide emergency supplies, even when the terrain is frightening for you as well.

The Adolescent and Intellectual Development

As children grow to maturity they change from being very concrete in their thinking during the first ten years, to being quite good at abstract thinking by age twenty. The ages of eleven to fourteen and fourteen upward are very critical intellectual transition periods. During the period from age eleven to fourteen the pre-adolescent is beginning to learn to think logically. In essence he is becoming a scientist. Discoveries are made and logical extensions of those discoveries are tried. The approach, however, is awkward and the person is unable to build tight arguments. This period is also marked by inconsistency and regressing back to concrete thought. By the time many adolescents reach age fourteen their abstract skills are getting much sharper. Muuss describes this period as follows: "An adolescent, unlike the child, is an individual who thinks beyond the present and forms theories about everything, delighting especially in consideration of that which is not (Piaget, 1947b: 148). He not only thinks beyond the present, but analytically reflects about his own thinking."[2]

This distinction between the thinking of children and the thinking of adults is highlighted in 1 Corinthians 13:11: *"When I was a child, I talked like a child, I thought like a child, I reasoned like a child. When I became a man, I put childish ways behind me."*

Abstract vs. Concrete Thinking Patterns

As a parent, you may read about these differences without really realizing the effect that they have on your ability to interact with your adolescent. Several potential areas of conflict can arise from these differences. For example, consider what happens if you relate to your adolescents as though they are capable of abstract thinking when in fact they are not. You may ask a specific question from which you expect them to reason, but they may never go beyond the question.

Melissa, age eleven, is asked the abstract question, "What will happen if you don't feed the horses?" She may be able to answer the question, but never go beyond that to realize that I am asking her to feed them because they are hungry right now. As an adult, I may become upset and wonder how she can ignore me when she knows the horses are hungry. Her behavior may be interpreted as laziness or stubbornness, when in fact the behavior is the product of her current intellectual stage.

If the parent becomes upset, the pre-adolescent will say, "I don't know what's bothering him. I didn't know he wanted me to feed the horses." During this period it is better to be quite specific about demands. Entering into abstract thinking with the person at other times, however, helps the adolescent develop in this area.

Battle of the Wits

Another area of conflict that may occur if you don't understand your adolescent's intellectual growth is what I call the Battle of the Wits. Adolescents love to match wits with their parents. This is the way they test and sharpen their new reasoning skills. Problems arise when parents take this stage too seriously and become emotionally involved in winning or losing.

My son Mark often says, "Dad, that doesn't make sense. Now just listen to me." From there he proceeds to show me logically why I am wrong and why he is right. If I am honest, I will recognize that sometimes he has some very good points to make. Often his conclusions are even right. I handle this best when I realize *I don't have to be right all* _the time._ Being honest with myself and with him is better than being right. If I am honest I find him more willing to listen to me and even to admit when he is wrong. How sweet it is to hear a sixteen-year-old say, "Oh yeah, I never thought about that."

Remember that the relationship will break down if you become emotionally involved with having to assert yourself as intellectually superior to your adolescent. If you want to see your teens smile, let them know when you notice how they are developing their ability to think. Secretly they will admire your ability and will be pleased when you notice that they are becoming as good at thinking as you are.

Recognizing that your teen is developing good logical skills does not mean that you will let them argue their way out of doing what you ask them to do. You are the parent and need to maintain the position of authority. However, this task is much easier if you acknowledge your teens' abilities, elicit their input, and consider their input in the decisions you make.

Some of our most joyful times with our teens have come when the three of them have tried to convince Sandy and me logically why we should do what they want rather than what we had planned. Sometimes we have changed our minds. Other times the discussions have ended amicably by Sandy or me saying, "Sorry guys, your reasoning is good, but this is one of those times when rank has its privilege."

Don't be afraid to interact with your teenagers on an intellectual level. They need that to help them grow, and you need it to develop your understanding of them. Dobson emphasizes the need for intellectual interaction between parent and teen by stating: "Knowing that adolescents often chafe under their lack of status in the adult world, I would offer this very important suggestion to the parents of a teenager: Treat him with genuine respect and dignity. Let your manner convey your acceptance of him as an individual, even aiming your conversation a year or two above his head."[3]

Conflicts over Motives

A third area of potential difficulty that may be avoided if you understand your teens' intellectual development is conflict over motives. Hearing a teenager say, "You hurt me and you did it on purpose!" or "You never want me to have fun!" is not uncommon. Parents also attribute motives by such statements as, "You are trying to destroy yourself," or "Why do you always try to make me look bad?" The ability to assign intention is an important intellectual skill which both adolescents and their parents need, but it often becomes a real stumbling block in relationships.

The problem in dealing with the *why* (motives) of behavior is that the *why* often becomes the focal point rather than the *what*. If my daughter gets home one hour past her curfew time I may wonder *why*. I may even think that she has purposely stayed out late because she is angry with me. However, this should not be my first concern. The first concern is the *what*. "You were one hour late and our agreement is that when you are one hour late you lose that amount of time the next time you go out." After we have agreed about this point, it might then be helpful to ask something like, "Do you think your being late had anything to do with the fact that we haven't talked through our disagreement?" If the teen identifies with your question, you can probably work it out. If she does not, then don't try to force the situation.

Allowing teenagers to discover their motives themselves is more effective than ascribing motives to them or forcing them to create a false motive in trying to answer the question, "Why did you do that?" In many instances a teenager will not be able to answer "Why?" until they have had time to reflect on it in a nonthreatening situation. I have found it more helpful to ask, "Is there anything you could have done differently?" or "Is there anything I could have done to have made it easier for you?" rather than, "Why did you do that?"

Adolescent Egocentrism

Another important aspect of the intellectual development of the adolescent is what has been called "adolescent egocentrism." During the period of adolescence teenagers revert back in some ways to the self-centeredness of childhood. In essence, their intellectual growth and newfound powers result in the world once more revolving around them. Adolescents believe that with their newfound ability to think they can change the world. They have little tolerance for the narrow thinking of parents who seek to hold them back. Adolescents also have a limited ability to take another person's point of view. This egocentrism is not a disease. It is simply a period they go through.

The research of David Elkind has revealed that adolescents manifest their egocentrism in two main ways. The first is through the presence of an "imaginary audience." For the adolescent, all the world is a stage and he is in the middle of it. Even though this idealism is crushed at times by parental rejection, ideas of greatness persist. Much of the attention-seeking behavior of adolescents traces back to their view of themselves as performers on the stage.

A second manifestation of egocentrism is the "personal fable." The personal fable includes the stories adolescents tell themselves about their importance. These stories often focus on power or even immortality. Jim stated, "Sometimes I believe that I could never die. I must have some very important work to do." A young woman imagines herself as a very successful race car driver. She has won races and received applause, money, and fame. The fact that she has never even driven the family car is inconsequential to her.

The aspect of intellectual growth may be very frightening to a conservative, reality-oriented parent. Let me say this stage is important to normal intellectual growth. If you have observed one of these characteristics, it doesn't mean your teenager is going crazy or that you are going crazy, either. This state will succumb to more mature thinking at some point. In order to help your teens in the maturation or normalization process you will need to stay close to them. The more they know they are like you in the positive sense, the more they will be able to give up their fantasies, which they secretly know are not totally believable.

Assumptive Realities

Elkind has also discussed another interesting aspect of adolescent intellectual development which he calls "assumptive realities." An assumptive reality is a belief the adolescent holds about how the world operates. In general, these views are based upon the adolescent's observations and reveal a great deal of cognitive conceit on the part of the adolescent. The teenager knows that things are a certain way because he knows it. There are two commonly held assumptive realities: (1) a belief that parents are benevolent and good-intentioned, and (2) a belief that the parent is not as smart as the adolescent. Some adolescents admit that they don't outwit their parents more just because they know that their parents are good. As a parent, I take great comfort in this balance.

In addition to the more generally held assumptive realities, there are assumptive realities which are often employed only in specific situations. Elkind explains how this happens.

This frequently occurs when the child does something he knows to be wrong. Although the child may be aware that he has committed a wrong he may also make some assumption about his behavior that excuses or exonerates his act so that he feels genuinely innocent. When he denies the action on the basis of this assumptive reality he is more than likely to infuriate the adult. Many toe-to-toe shouting matches between parent and child follow upon the child's denial of guilt and the parent's adamant demand that the child confess his misdeed. At such times the parent fails to appreciate that for the child an assumptive reality is the truth.[4]

In situations such as this the parent needs to keep the focus on the *what* and not become overly concerned about correcting the assumptive reality. As one psychologist has pointed out, these realities will inevitably lose their believability for the adolescent.

Hopefully this discussion on how adolescents develop intellectually has stimulated you to learn even more about your teenager. The Psalmist has said, *"I am fearfully and wonderfully made"* (Psalm 139:14). This applies to all of us—parents and teens. Your challenge as a parent is to focus on the wonderfulness of your teenager as God's creation, and not upon the fearful aspects.

One of the greatest things about parenting teenagers is that they are exciting social creatures. During the adolescent years they become more than mind, more than body. They become social. They are in transition from being social extensions of their parents to being their own persons in relationships.

During the adolescent years the social focus of the adolescent is on the peer group. The group of friends becomes the catalyst for much of the identity formation that is taking place. Instead of identifying themselves as extensions of their parents, teenagers see themselves as part of a group. Dacey points out: "The teenager peer group is seen as a relatively safe place for adolescents to take a long look at themselves, prior to deciding what kind of adult they wish to be."[5]

The teenage peer group results in new patterns of behavior, new channels of communication, and new desires for autonomy. Authority is rejected and traditional values may be sidelined at least for a time.

Socially, the adolescent period prepares the teenager to be able to leave father and mother and be prepared for his own independent life. There is a transfer of dependence from one person or party to another. In other words, the parents have to be replaced so that at a later date they can assume their proper place. Berzonsky elaborates by noting: "Adolescents become aware that their friends are not impressed by the fact that they enjoy derived status within their family. To gain favor with their peers, therefore, some adolescents transfer their allegiance. For instance, a youth may begin to conform to the wishes of peers rather than parents."[6]

Often the breaking away process is misunderstood by the parents and is interpreted as withdrawal of love or rejection. This is not the case. The love is still there. It is just being expressed within the context of independence and new relationships. The teenager needs the opportunity to earn his own status and to stand with others so that eventually he can stand independently. Smooth breaking away is aided by parents who expect and reward responsible behavior and allow the teenager to make mistakes without rejection.

I believe there are four social developmental tasks for the adolescent which parents should seek to facilitate. Breaking away is the first and may in some ways encompass the others. The last three all have to do with friendship. Teenagers need to learn to be friends with same-sex peers, persons of the opposite sex, and adults other than their parents. I believe these three friendship patterns are crucial to making the social transaction to adulthood. Learning to relate closely and openly to persons in each of these categories becomes a part of the resolution of the identity crisis. Think for a moment about how important it is for you to be able to say, when asked, who you are. I am a friend. I have close friends. I have friends of the same sex. I have friends of the opposite sex. I have adult friends. When I am an adult I know I will have friends.

The Adolescent and Moral and Spiritual Development

This area is too important to be tucked away at the end of a chapter so it has been given a careful treatment in chapters 7 and 8. My purpose in the paragraphs that follow is to prepare the reader for those chapters by highlighting some of the processes that take place during adolescence which affect both spiritual and moral growth. Each of the three areas of development we have discussed up to this point affect the capacity for spiritual and moral development. The physical, intellectual, and social aspects of development are instrumental in determining the type of values and beliefs which will emerge.

Factors Affecting Development

The first influence upon spiritual and moral development during adolescence is the physical development of the teenager. As the body takes on more importance as a focal point for the teenager's self-acceptance, new temptations arise and new areas for discussion become apparent. Teenagers must decide how they are going to use this newfound source of power and pleasure. Pleasure awareness puts them in conflict with existing morals and with their spiritual belief system. The Apostle Paul's awareness of the temptations associated with physical development prompted him to warn those who were young. *"Flee the evil desires of youth, and pursue righteousness, faith, love and peace, along with those who call on the Lord out of a pure heart"* (2 Timothy 2:22).

With new capacities for abstract thought come new opportunities to question existing standards and to develop personal standards. This process of challenging the existing standards has both a positive and negative side. The positive side is that when standards and beliefs are challenged, the resulting conclusions are often internalized in a more permanent way than ever before. The person who thinks through what he believes sometimes changes some of his beliefs, but he also holds those things he does believe more strongly. The faith of our fathers becomes a personal faith.

On the negative side the thinking through process may result in rebellion, or in at least a temporary retreat from previously accepted standards or beliefs. New ideas will be tried and old ideas will be tested. In some cases this may mean that significant changes from pre-adolescent positions will result. This is often a very trying period for the parent who would like to see things stay constant.

Not all changes during adolescence are movements away from traditional, moral, or spiritual values. The idealism which characterizes adolescence may also bring many persons to personal faith and to a conservative value system. One thing is certain: Changes of some type will occur and new ideas and behaviors will be tested.

Spiritual and moral development is also affected by the social development of the teenager. As the process of breaking away occurs, the peer group rather than the family becomes the focal point for spiritual and moral decisions. This does not mean that family values will be abandoned. It means they will be questioned even if the adolescent's peer group comes from families with similar values. The thrust will be upon questioning rather than upon complying.

Often teenagers select a peer group with values quite different from their parents, as though they are trying to be negatively influenced. This frightens many parents, who respond by trying to control friendships. This in turn results in further rebellion by the teenager, who doesn't feel trusted. In some cases, however, the opportunity to see the other side helps adolescents to see the value of their current beliefs or values. Obviously, this is a complex process that seems to be resolved most satisfactorily when parents maintain contact while allowing their teenager to wrestle with the issues.

Learning to Empathize
One of the most important developmental tasks related to the

spiritual and moral area is the development of empathy. The person with empathy is able to feel what others are feeling. In other words, an empathetic person can put himself into the shoes of another person. Empathy is necessary if standards of moral conduct are to be more than just self-serving. If an individual is unable to see how others feel he will not consider the needs of others in making decisions. Empathy development is in part an intellectual process. The adolescent must be able mentally to take the role of the other person.

Empathy also involves such social skills as listening and give-and-take, which result in greater understanding of others. Parents can help in this process by sharing their own feelings without trying to produce guilt. They can also help the teenager identify his own feelings. Development of empathy is a prerequisite for practicing the so-called Golden Rule. Spiritual and moral development is a sorting process. It is a time of evaluation of standards and of trying on new ideas. It is a time of becoming spiritual or moral rather than just going through the motions because parents and others seem to be doing them. Adolescence is not a problem in this area. It is an opportunity.

Changing with the Teens

There are many developmental changes which occur during adolescence. The one thing you should count on is that you can't count on anything, not even your child's looks. If you are bothered by all of these changes, think how overwhelming it must be for your teenager. The task for parents is to discover a new role that will enable them to be a part of the solution rather than just an extension of the problem.

Basketball coaches stress the importance of a team being able to make the *transition* from defense to offense and vice-versa as the game progresses. In a very real sense, this is our challenge as parents during the teen years. We must change and make transitions because we are dealing with people who are changing and making transitions. Deliberate, thoughtful change will enable you to stay with your teenagers, and as they see you change they will be able to stay close to you.

Footnotes

[1]Arthur T. Jersild, Judith S. Brook and David W. Brook, *The Psychology of Adolescence,* 3d ed. (New York: Macmillan Publishing Co., Inc., 1978), p. 56.

[2]Rolf E. Muuss, *Theories of Adolescence* (New York: Random House, 1975), p. 192.

[3]James Dobson, *Hide or Seek* (Old Tappan, N.J.: Fleming H. Revell, 1974), p. 111.

[4]David Elkind, *Children and Adolescents: Interpretative Essays on Jean Piaget,* 2d ed. (New York: Oxford Press, 1974), p. 86.

[5]John Stewart Dacey, *Adolescents Today* (Santa Monica: Goodyear Publishing Co., Inc., 1979), p. 183.

[6]Michael D. Berzonsky, *Adolescent Development* (New York: Macmillan Publishing Co., Inc., 1981), p. 299.

Chapter 3

Dealing with the Problems of Control

Who is the boss and why do I care?

Former President Harry S. Truman made famous the phrase, "The buck stops here." Loosely translated, this phrase means, "I'll take the responsibility." In parent-teen relationships it appears that everyone wants to be in control, but no one wants to take responsibility. In our society responsibility is given to the parent. Control, however, does not always go with responsibility.

A part of the developmental process discussed in the previous chapter involves the adolescent's desire for control. Adolescents test their parents to see what having control is like. This creates deep conflicts for many families, particularly if the parent does not understand that a part of the process of growing up is to try to take charge.

A Losing Battle

Often this struggle results in the changing of roles, with adolescents acting like parents and parents responding like insecure children. Some parents become desperate as they try to maintain control. They have a strong need to be the boss. Other parents soon tire of the hassle and remove themselves from the struggle. "Why do I care?" they say, while barely masking their deep hurt. Ginott describes the uselessness of trying to struggle with one's teenagers.

> There is no way to win a war with our own children. Time and energy are on their side. Even if we mobilize and win a battle, they can strike back with awesome vengeance. They can become defiant and delinquent, or passive and neurotic. They

have all the weapons: If enraged enough, a teenage boy can steal a car and a teenage girl can get pregnant. They can worry us to death or put us to public shame.[1]

In its most brutal form this struggle results in both parent and teenager trying to belittle the other in order to assume superiority in the battle for control. There is a very real sense in which no one can win this vicious battle.

Recently one of my sons said, "You can't make me do that." My fighting spirit started to surface and I wanted to show him otherwise. I gained control quickly enough to realize that in some ways he was right. Short of brutality, I couldn't make him do anything. Even then I am living on borrowed time because as he gets older and stronger, I get older and weaker.

I stopped my defensive response and rephrased it. "You are right," I said. "I can't make you do anything. I can, however, ask you to do things and expect that you will do them." He grinned and said, "Okay."

Winning by Helping Your Teen Gain Personal Power, Respect, and Responsibility

The issue was not that my son wanted to defeat me. The issue was that he wanted me to recognize him as a person and as a person of strength. He knows that rank has its privilege, but that does not stop him from testing the limits. Parents need to understand that this is a part of the process of growing up. Your teenagers will try to control situations mentally, socially, and physically. A wise parent will not be intimidated by this, but will help the teenager gain a sense of personal power while at the same time demanding respect and holding the teenager responsible for his behavior.

Relationships break down when parents get pulled into a struggle for control and try to show the teenager how insignificant he is. This usually results in an intensified struggle and a lot of anger and revenge. The parent's responsibility is to discover how to avoid this problem. The parent has both the most to gain and the most to lose.

I followed up with my son by saying, "It is true that I can't make you do anything now, and you can't make me do anything. We have a choice. We can either fight each other, or cooperate with each other." We don't always cooperate, but we both know that when we do cooperate we each get more of our needs met. Learning to cooperate is a superior option to learning to control.

Recently I criticized my older son for being mouthy. At times I felt that he was trying to control his mother and me by talk that bordered on disrespect. When I challenged him, he said, "I may be mouthy, but you have to admit I'm obedient." I laughed and said, "That's true. I guess I can tolerate a little mouth for obedience." He is learning verbal power. His statement was his way of expressing submission even though he pushes us at times.

Through personal experience and reading I have discovered a number of principles that are very useful in dealing with the problems of control. They are not presented here as the final word, but as thought stimulators to help you more effectively face the control issues with your adolescent.

Allow the Child to Develop a Sense of Personal Power

Social scientists agree that one of the compelling developmental tasks for the maturing human being is the quest for a sense of personal power. The developing human being is in the process of being changed from a totally dependent creature at birth, to a mature adult who is expected to have the physical and psychological resources to care not only for self but also for others. Children compare themselves with adults and long for the power which they see adults exhibiting.

Struggling for Personal Power with Your Teen

Power struggles between children and their parents may be instigated by the children as early as the first year of life. By the time the child is age three, parents are usually well aware that the little darling has a mind of his own. During the teen years when the child is growing rapidly both physically and mentally, the adolescent tests his new-found strength against his standard of power—the parents. This may take the form of mental one-up-manship, demonstrations of physical superiority, or struggles with authority. My thirteen-year-old loves to tell me how to do things. His emerging competency gives him a sense of power, particularly when he knows he is superior to me in a specific area.

The quest for power can be either a source of blessing or a curse for the parents and the teenagers, depending on how it is worked out in the relationship between the two. If the parent views the process as normal and strives to help the youngster gain a sense of power, the outcome will usually be positive. On the other hand, if the parent views the process as a personal threat and fights to continually demonstrate superiority over the teenager, the relationship between the two will be damaged and the parent will ultimately lose control and influence with the teenager.

Developing Personal Power in Your Teen

Giving power to your teenager does not mean that you have forsaken your God-given responsibility or that you allow your teenager to run over you. Power can be given without the parent losing authority. Power is not a matter of heavy-handedness. It is a matter of openness and expression of desire for your teenager to gain a sense of power.

I want my teenagers to know that they are powerful people, but I also want them to realize that this God-given power or ability carries with it a sense of stewardship. I want to use my power to help them become more powerful persons and I want them to learn that the most powerful person in the world was a servant. The greatest power is the ability to give up power for the sake of others. In other words I want them to be like Christ. Paul describes Christ's attitude well in Philippians 2:6-8: *"Who, being in very nature God, did not consider equality with God something to be grasped, but made himself nothing, taking the very nature of a servant, being made in human likeness. And being found in appearance as a man, he humbled himself and became obedient to death—even death on a cross!"*

A sense of personal power begins to develop when the following things happen:

1. *The teenager realizes that he is really valued by God and his parents.* Self worth is not only strengthened by understanding divine revelation, but by sensing parental support. As a teen realizes his importance in the eyes of others, he will develop a balanced sense of personal power.

2. *The teenager realizes that God, the great Enabler, did not pass him by.* As a youngster I remember the chant, "When God passed out brains, you thought He said trains, and you missed yours." Teenagers need to realize that God didn't miss them.

3. *The teenager is helped to become good at something he enjoys.* Physical beauty, athletic prowess, or even academic success must not be the only acceptable standards for success. Not all people will be "A" students when the teacher grades on the curve.

4. *The teenager is accepted.* There is no greater source of power than to know that your ideas and your dreams are taken seriously. Parents spend too much time bringing teenagers back to reality and not enough time sharing their dreams.

5. *The teenager has the opportunity to exercise responsibility.* I heard a young man say, "Sometime I would just like to be the boss of something." Parents can grant that right. It will increase the youngster's sense of personal power and it will also increase the power that the parent has with the teenager.

6. *The teenager is shown extravagant love.* My father is not one to go overboard in overt expressions of affection, but he is sensitive. One time during my youth when I felt power as the result of his love was when he did something for me that he couldn't afford. I had been bitterly disappointed when a person who had promised to loan me a gun for the opening day of pheasant season suddenly and unexplainably withheld the gun when I went to pick it up. I felt totally helpless and rejected as I slowly walked home. There were no stores open and the opening of the season was only hours away.

When my dad realized the situation he called a merchant at his home and arranged to meet him at his store which was ten miles away. Two hours later I was the owner of a very simple but adequate gun. It was the best gun ever made because even when it missed the target it said, "Earl Wilson, my son, has worth." Dad may have been a little extravagant, but his actions helped me to feel power and to know that the love of my Heavenly Father is also extravagant.

When teenagers are given power by their parents, they don't have to struggle for it, and the problems of control become less significant. This is a hard lesson to learn because our human nature wants to grasp control, even when the grasping results in less control in the long run.

Don't Take Out Other Power Frustrations on Your Teenager

The concept of the pecking order is very real to most people today. Much of our social system is based upon it. The people with the most power take precedence over people with less power who lord it over the people with the least power. Jesus spoke out against such a system in the Gospel of Luke, but unfortunately the pecking order still creeps into many of our churches today.

When he noticed how the guests picked the places of honor at the table, he told them this parable: "When someone invites you to a wedding feast, do not take the place of honor, for a person more distinguished than you may have been invited. If so, the host who invited both of you will come and say to you, 'Give this man your seat.' Then, humiliated, you will have to take the least important place. But when you are invited, take the lowest place, so that when your host comes, he will say to you, 'Friend, move up to a better place.' Then you will be honored in the presence of all your fellow guests. For everyone who exalts himself will be humbled, and he who humbles himself will be exalted" (Luke 14:7-11).

As an adult I sometimes feel that I am abused by others. My sense of personal power is frustrated by others who lord it over me or by my failure to reach my goals. The temptation is to take my frustration out on others, even my family, when things have not gone as I would have liked them to go. As a parent, I need to resist this temptation if I am going to be effective with my teenagers. Otherwise I will force unnecessary struggles over control which have no real purpose other than to try to salve my own battered ego. Such attempts always fail and usually result in a deeper sense of failure on my part as a parent. I only set myself up to lose the battle with my teenager, thus adding to my sense of frustration.

Sometimes when I have felt severely defeated, I have taken the occasion to share those feelings with the family, and to warn them that I may not treat them the way I should until I get my feelings resolved. Usually they have been very supportive in this process and the love shared has become the therapy I needed. I don't expect them to fix things for me or to feel sorry for me. I just want them to know why I may be acting poorly so that they will not assume that it is their fault or take responsibility for my problem.

Bullies are usually highly frustrated people who find someone weaker than themselves to take out their frustrations on. The worst kind of bullying is to take out those frustrations on family members. This only produces guilt, not personal power.

Give Respect and Expect Respect

Ephesians 5 and 6 is a well known passage of Scripture that speaks to three sets of relationships: husband-wife, parent-child, and master-slave (which in our culture could be considered employer-employee). The passage begins with a challenge to *"be imitators of God."* Then in 5:21 Paul states, *"Submit to one another out of reverence for Christ."* In the verses that follow, the way each party is to submit to the other is described, such as how husbands are to submit by loving their wives.

How are parents and children to submit to each other? Children, which include teenagers, are to submit by obeying their parents *and* by honoring them. They are to give respect to their parents. Parents, on the other hand, are to bring them up in the *"training and instruction of the Lord"* (Ephesians 6:4). In this way parents show respect for their children.

This seems simple, but if each is giving respect, each will be respected. The problem comes when demanding respect becomes more important than giving respect. A good exercise for parents is to think through some of the ways that their teenagers need to be respected. Three important areas of respect are discussed in Chapter 4. These areas are respect for abilities, plans, and privacy. Another important area is respect of the teenager's rights. We will consider it here because of its close relationship to control.

The area of rights can best be illustrated by the right to finish what you start without being interrupted. When my children request something of me, I always respond, "Just a minute." When I request something of them and they say, "Just a minute," I say "Not just a minute. You do it now because I said so." If you think this is a dual standard, you are right.

I need to realize that my teenager has as much right as I do to finish an activity before responding. If I fail to recognize this, I will set up a struggle for control which will not be good for either of us. It is good to ask, "Is there any reason why you can't do it right now?" If there is, then choose to be patient. If there isn't, then let them know that responding now would be helpful to you. This seems like such a simple process, but it has helped me to avoid numerous struggles for control. The process itself encourages mutual respect. Respect is a prerequisite for control and mutual support.

Don't Sacrifice the War in Order to Win a Battle

One of my good friends who, with his wife, has raised four beautiful people, said to me, "The hardest decision a parent has to make with teenagers is to decide which battles are important enough to fight. You can't deal with every potential conflict that arises. You just don't have enough energy." His comment reminded me of the adage about winning a battle but losing the war.

Knowing Which Battles to Fight
Conduct the following experiment and you will know what I mean. Time yourself for one half hour. During this time listen to your teen-

ager or teenagers and make a mark on a piece of paper each time you hear something you don't like or something that causes you to feel irritated. Here are some things I marked: They played the music too loud, they insulted one another, they left a job half finished, they tied up the telephone, one raised his voice at me, another complained about our discipline of a younger child, and there were numerous negative statements.

As I thought about this list, I realized it would take hours of time to try to deal with even half of the list. In the meantime a new list would develop. I cannot effectively confront all the things I would like to control. In fact, some of the irritations I would like to control probably aren't important at all.

I can, however, prioritize some areas where I would like to make an impact and work on them. For example, I might decide to concentrate on helping one or more of the teenagers to respond more positively and to complain less. I won't accomplish this by nagging every time they complain. I will be successful, however, if I make a game of it and encourage them instead of continually exhorting. Picking one thing at a time to try to change is usually best. You will be more effective and your teenager will not feel like you are putting down everything they do.

Developing a Strategic Battle Plan

If you have been trying to fight all the battles at once and feel like you are losing the war, I suggest that you retreat from the front lines long enough to think about what you really want to accomplish with your teenager. In the military, "R and R" (rest and relaxation) is recognized as a must in order to prevent battle fatigue. This is great advice for parents, as well.

John White has pointed out that although parents need peace they cannot expect uninterrupted tranquility. Disruption and conflict come with the job. The very fight for tranquility results in a struggle for control that cannot be attained. Peace, which is the fruit of the Holy Spirit, must be acknowledged and accepted. Peace is not attainable through striving or trying to control. White writes: "There are times when you can and should insist that your needs and even your wishes take priority over your children's demands. But if your peace depends on so controlling events that nothing gets out of hand but that everything remains in its place, then either you or your children are going to be in trouble. Probably your tension will rise till you explode."[2]

If control is an issue between you and your teenager, do not be afraid to draw some lines. They expect that of you. However, lines are more carefully followed when they are distinct and when there are not so many of them that they can't be traced. The war for control with teenagers is best won with carefully selected, strategic plans, not with all our effort on every possible battle front.

Strive for Compliance—Not for Joyful Subservience

When parents complain that they can't control their teenagers, I frequently ask the question, "Does he do what you ask him to do?" The answer is often, "Yeah, but . . . ! He does it, but I don't like the way he does it. It's his attitude, you see." When I pursue the issue I find that parents often believe that teenagers should not only be compliant, but should also be delighted over the opportunity to comply. We have stressed proper attitudes to the point that we often ignore the fact that the teenager is quite compliant even if he or she isn't showing a big smile.

There are hundreds of things that I do each week because I have to do them or because someone is demanding that I do them. The important thing is not whether I like doing them or not, but that I get them done. I have learned that I might as well enjoy doing these things. Otherwise I will just make myself miserable.

I did not learn this attitude, however, by being harassed about my bad attitude. I learned it by watching the attitudes of my mom and dad, and by seeing them turn undesirable tasks into tolerable and even pleasant experiences. They told me on occasion that I might as well enjoy what I had to do. At other times they became stern and said, "Shape up your attitude! You don't have to be abusive just because you don't like what you are doing."

The point is my parents did not try to control my attitude. They tried to lead me to discover the importance of a good attitude. They knew that a good attitude was important for me. They did not demand my good attitude for themselves. They did, however, expect me to do what they asked even if I didn't like it. Once again, their positive example was the most important thing in my attitude development.

When my teenagers complain, I often agree with them that I don't like some things either. We don't have to like it. We just have to do it. At times my teenagers have been open to my sharing how I move to the positive. For example, I relate that I do an undesirable task—like work extra long hours—while thinking of the fun we will have on vacation. Or I help clean the house when I realize that Sandy will not have to work so hard that day. The important thing is receptivity. Some days the teenagers are in a place to listen. When they are, sharing is helpful. When I see that they aren't in a mood to listen, I ask, "You don't want a lecture today, do you?" Even that will help build the relationship and make them more receptive for the next time.

Allow God to Use Your Teenagers to Help You Learn Humility

I am writing this section of the chapter with the full realization that by the time you finish reading it you may want to burn this book or throw it at me. I, too, resist the idea of learning from my children, especially from conflicts with my children, but when I look back I see that it has happened.

Teenagers do keep us humble, but there is a difference between being humbled (embarrassed) and learning humility in the sense described in Philippians 2.

Experiencing Joy in Humiliation

John White reflects the humbling experience that many parents go through. He writes: " 'Haven't I fed and clothed them?' some parents say. 'Didn't I bring them into the world? Who paid for their education? Who worked their fingers to the bone so that they could get extra training in sports, in music, in horseback riding? And look what they've done for me. . . .' "[3]

What have they done to you? Have you suffered? Who says that suffering is not a part of life? Sometimes the work of parenting demands suffering and humiliation, just as the work of Jesus placed demands on Him. *"Let us fix our eyes on Jesus,"* the writer of Hebrews urges us, for He is *"the author and perfecter of our faith, who for the joy set before him endured the cross, scorning its shame, and sat down at the right hand of the throne of God"* (Hebrews 12:2).

Interestingly, this passage depicts Jesus as experiencing both joy and shame in accomplishing what He came to do. My experience tells me that as a parent I too will experience both joy and humiliation. If I am ready to accept this I will be much more content to deal with each situation as it comes up without being a martyr.

Experiencing Growth through Humiliation

Notice the next verse: *"consider him who endured such opposition from sinful men, so that you will not grow weary and lose heart"* (Hebrews 12:3).

We may not always think of our children as "sinful men," but they do have sin natures and they do sin against God and against us. We are not to grow weary and lose heart. Don't take the power struggle personally. You will be hurt, but you will survive, and you will experience joy in the process if you allow yourself to remain open.

Solomon described this process wisely when he said that, *"As iron sharpens iron, so one man sharpens another"* (Proverbs 27:17). The relationship between parent and teenager is a very intense metal-to-metal relationship. Both parent and teenager will be permanently affected by the interaction they share. Even though interaction can result in growth and shaping, it is often bittersweet. The key is keeping your focus on the sweet. The bitter will take care of itself.

When you are brought to the end of yourself, as often happens when you struggle over issues such as control, you are then in a position to let God show you how He wants to work in you and in the life of your teenager. Often we do our greatest work when we realize that we cannot maintain control and thus commit the control of the teenager to God. Our humble release of them may allow them to ease up in the struggle to control us. It is a paradox, but often we have to become humble enough to give up before we win.

Giving up, however, is not giving up your role or your responsibilities, but giving up your demanding that the adolescent turn out a certain way. This is illustrated by Jesus' words: *"Whoever finds his life will lose it, and whoever loses his life for my sake will find it"* (Matthew 10:39).

I have heard teenagers say that the problem with parents is they are not willing to learn. One young man said, "Even if I'm absolutely right my dad and mom won't listen. They have to have it their way." These parents could learn much from God through their children. They would find that in being more humble and open to their teenagers they would "find" their lives and be more effective.

The Control and Freedom Paradox

Parents often assume that if they are to be free they must have greater control of their teenagers. The teenagers, on the other hand, assume that true freedom results when they feel free from the control of their parents. The confusion comes when we think either that freedom is lack of control or is total control. Freedom is neither. *Freedom is*

the ability to act in accordance with your will. In other words, freedom
is being who you are without the facade.

Teenage Rebellion

Young people usually want to be respectful and they usually want to
do what is right. Sometimes their desire to please parents is even too
strong. That is the way they are. Rebellion is not an attempt on their
part to take control. Rebellion is a reaction that comes when the control pressure from the parents is so great that teenagers feel they can't
act in accordance with their will. That is, they feel they can't please
their parents or do what is right. When parents recognize this and back
off, the teenager is then able to make decisions that allow him to feel
free while at the same time giving the parents a sense of control.

Why do building codes require that public buildings be equipped
with exit doors with "panic bars"—long bars that release the door
when you press against them? The answer is quite simple. When
emergencies like fires occur, people press against each other to get out
of the building. Hundreds have died because the pressure has been so
great that those nearest the door have not been able to act in accordance with their will to turn the door knob. Many lives would have been
spared if those in the back would have taken the pressure off those
who needed to turn the doorknob. This is analogous to the need to
take the pressure off the teenager so that he is able to think clearly and
act accordingly. No one wants to die in a fire, but some do when they
panic.

Freedom and Control in Collision

Freedom and control seem almost paradoxical. The harder you
strive to control, the less freedom you feel. The other side of the coin is
that, when given freedom, teenagers are often less insistent on control.
There is another interesting fact about freedom and control which is illustrated in Figure 2. The problem the figure points out is that as parents get older they have a continuing need for control, but as teenagers
get older they have a greater desire for freedom. This creates a natural
collision course unless both parents and teenagers understand what is
happening.

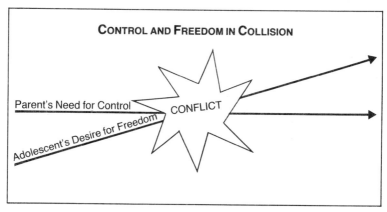

Figure 2

The solution to this conflict is twofold. First, parents need to turn loose. Children are on temporary loan from God, and the amount of time the parents need to exercise strict control is quite limited. It begins early and ends early, somewhere in the teen years. Second, adolescents need to honor their parents and carefully consider their wishes without just pacifying them. The teenager needs to learn to assert his needs and desires without falling into the trap of disrespect. At this point the roles are reversed. Early in life children ask, "Why do I have to do that?" or "Why can't I do this?" Later they ask, "Why don't you do what I want you to do?" or "Why aren't you doing what I think is right?"

Who is the boss? And why do I care? These are the questions with which we started. The answers were quite simple. No one needs to be boss even though the buck does stop with the parents. Both parents and adolescents must be responsible to and respectful of the other party. As parents, we care because we love our teenagers and want to raise them properly. The error to be avoided is too much control with too little relationship. When this happens, whatever influence is there will soon be eroded.

Footnotes

[1]Haim G. Ginott, *Between Parent and Teenager* (New York: Avon Books, 1969), p. 127.
[2]John White, *Parents in Pain* (Downers Grove, Ill.: InterVarsity Press, 1979), p. 172.
[3]White, pp. 165-66.

Chapter 4

Zeroing in on Needs

I'm confused, God! Who needs what?

Understanding the needs of our adolescents is one of the greatest challenges that we face. In fact, if you are honest with yourself, you will recognize that you have difficulty understanding your own needs, let alone those of someone else. Psychologist Henry Murray developed an entire theory of human personality based on the concept of human needs. This is what he says in part about them.

Each need is characteristically accompanied by a particular feeling or emotion and tends to use certain modes . . . to further its trend. It may be weak or intense, momentary or enduring. But usually it persists and gives rise to a certain course of overt behavior (or fantasy), which . . . changes the initiating circumstance in such a way as to bring about an end situation which stills (appeases or satisfies) the organism. [1]

Identify Each Other's Needs

Parents have two basic challenges in this area: identifying the needs of the teenager, and identifying their own needs with regard to the teenager. When both of these challenges are met, then the possibility of meeting the needs of the teenager becomes a reality. You cannot meet needs that you cannot see, and you cannot meet needs from a vacuum. If you are devoid of having your own needs met, you will not be able to consistently reach out to your teenager.

I have a strong need, for example, for uninterrupted sleep because I

53

am in an early morning schedule. I really don't like telephone calls after 11 p.m. On the other hand, my daughter may have a high need for flexibility. She cannot always anticipate everything she is going to do in an evening. On one occasion she called me after 11 p.m. to ask if she could go out for pizza with her friends after a school activity. I was irritated, grouchy, and not very flexible. She felt that her needs were not being met and I was certain that mine were being overlooked as well.

A day or so later we sat down to talk the situation through and discovered some workable solutions. If she wants to ask for an extension on her curfew, she is to do so before my bedtime. Otherwise the answer is "No." Whenever possible, she tries to anticipate activities so that she can let me know ahead of time. We have encouraged her to make good decisions within her need for flexibility. The most important part of the process was talking the situation through so that the possible source of irritation was diminished.

Identify the Needs of Your Teenager

We will now turn our attention to six basic needs that teenagers have. This list is only slightly different from the needs which parents often have. Teenagers and adults aren't really that different from each other. It just seems that way at times. As each need is discussed, I will attempt to give suggestions or ask questions that will help the reader focus on identifying the need and communicating to the teenager in such a way as to try to meet the need.

Please note that I said *try.* You may do all the right things and still be unsuccessful at times. Teenagers and parents both need to be receptive if their needs are to be met. We all need to cooperate with the attempts of others to meet our needs. You need to do things that your teenager *likes,* but only the teenager can choose to be *happy.* Keeping this fact in mind will help you focus on the process of reaching out, rather than getting hung up on the product of a fulfilled teenager. Keep doing the right things for the right reasons, because your teenager needs that, and sooner or later you will find the channel open. Let's look now at the six ways to meet your teen's basic needs.

1. Everybody Needs Love

But eagerly desire the greater gifts. And now I will show you the most excellent way. If I speak in the tongues of men and of

angels, but have not love, I am only a resounding gong or a
clanging cymbal. If I have the gift of prophecy and can fathom all
mysteries and all knowledge, and if I have a faith that can move
mountains, but have not love, I am nothing. If I give all I possess
to the poor and surrender my body to the flames, but have not
love, I gain nothing (1 Corinthians 12:31-13:3).

Love is easy to talk about and hard to understand. Love is highly
needed and sparingly received. It can be misinterpreted, misappro-
priated, or just plain misused. Not all love needs are the same. Loving
is an individualized process. All teenagers do not experience parental
love in the same way. Parents, too, have certain behaviors that are
perceived as love from the teenager while other attempts by the teenager to communicate love are rejected. The key is to get on the same
wavelength.

What does parental love mean to a teenager? How do teenagers
know when they are loved by their parents? What are some of the
ways parents try to love that don't work? I have asked these questions
to a number of teenagers and am happy to share the responses that I
have received.

Communicating Love to Your Teen

Teenagers report that they know they are loved when one or more
of the following conditions are met: when parents work to provide for
them; when parents listen and don't lecture; when parents treat them
like they have brains (I think this means respecting their intelligence);
when parents do things for them without constantly reminding them of
the sacrifices they are making; when parents treat them like adults; and
finally when parents allow them some freedom. This list is not all inclu-
sive, but it does provide us with some insight into loving our teenagers.

These key elements seem to be related to accepting the teenager as
a bona fide person. When parents are patient, kind, trusting, and positive in their attitude, this is seen by the teenager as love. This is not too
surprising when you read 1 Corinthians 13:4-7, which is the heart of
the love chapter: "Love is patient, love is kind. It does not envy, it does
not boast, it is not proud. It is not rude, it is not self-seeking, it is not
easily angered, it keeps no record of wrongs. Love does not delight in
evil but rejoices with the truth. It always protects, always trusts, always
hopes, always perseveres."

Failing to Communicate Love

Now let's look for a moment at things parents may do that teenagers perceive as unloving. The top of the list is *not respecting their privacy*. Reading mail without asking, listening in on the telephone, or other attempts to invade the teenager's world are all seen as the highest evidence that love is absent. One girl said, "I could never forgive my mother for reading my diary. That is the most unloving thing a parent could do."

A second action that teenagers see as unloving is *any form of putting them down*. Teenagers are very sensitive to having people make fun of them, particularly parents. You make light of something your teenager has done or use him as a source of conversation very innocently. The problem is that your innocent action is seen as a put down or as a betrayal of confidence. You cannot be too careful in this area. Even when you think you *might* have said something that could be perceived as a put down, go to your teenager and ask for forgiveness. By the way, when you ask your teenager for forgiveness, don't bother with all the rationalization. Be straightforward. Admit your error without qualification. In doing this, you will model taking responsibility for your actions to your teenager, and this straightforward apology will communicate love to your teenager. We don't want them to rationalize, so why should we?

A third source of communication of lack of love by the parent is *trying to make them be something they don't want to be*. We call this manipulation or blackmail. This is love with strings attached. John Powell calls it conditional love. One young man said, "My parents are always trying to get me to do things their way. They say it's for my own good but that's a bunch of bunk. I feel used! They want me to do things to make them feel better. I don't even know whether they care about me at all." This emotional tirade is typical of how angry teenagers become when they feel that real love is being replaced by the sham of manipulation.

John Powell has clearly stated that we must replace the counterfeit expression which we have discussed with the message of unconditional love.

> The essential message of unconditional love is one of liberation: You can be whoever you are, express all your thoughts and feelings with absolute confidence. You do not have to be fearful that love will be taken away. You will not be punished for your openness or honesty. There is no admission price to my love, no rental fees or installment payments to be made. There may be days when disagreements and disturbing emotions may come between us. There may be times when psychological or physical

miles may lie between us. But I have given you the word of my commitment. I have set my life on a course. I will not go back on my word to you. So feel free to be yourself, to tell me of your negative and positive reactions, of your warm and cold feelings. I cannot always predict my reactions or guarantee my strength, but one thing I do know and I do want you to know: I will not reject you! I am committed to your growth and happiness. I will always love you.[2]

How is your love life with your teenager? Spend time around them so that you will have opportunities to say, "I love you" both in words and deeds that they can accept as a true message of love. You will hear their love messages coming back to you, especially if you are willing to put up with some of the static in the airways.

2. Accept What You Cannot Always Understand

Have you ever been in a room with a group of people and somehow felt that you didn't belong? Teenagers feel that way much of the time, even in their own homes. They do not feel rejected. They just don't feel accepted. There is a difference. Rejection is usually overt and obvious. When you are rejected you know it. When lack of acceptance is present, it's not so much what the parents say, as it is what they don't say. Jill said, "My parents never acknowledge any of the things I do for them. It's like they expect it of me. They seem more interested in me as a slave than as a daughter."

Allow Them to Make Mistakes

The greatest single detriment to the communication of acceptance to the teenager seems to be in the area of correction. You take your responsibilities as a parent seriously. You want your teenagers to be successful and you long to see them mature physically, emotionally, and intellectually. The question is: What can you do to aid in the maturation process? Many parents choose correction. Each time the teenager gets off the track the parent reminds him of where he should be. The teenager obviously does not feel accepted. Ron reported, "My parents correct me so much, sometimes I wonder if I could ever do anything that they would think was okay." Acceptance stresses letting a person make mistakes, and watching him recover and grow. Acceptance says, "I know you will get where you want to be."

Allow Them to Be Different

Young people often choose to be different as a means of testing the acceptance of parents and peers. They may wear their hair long or insist on wearing torn or worn out jeans. They want to know if they are accepted or if people only value stylish hair or nice clothes. Wise parents will avoid the trap of caring what people think of them as parents, and will show acceptance to their teenager despite differences. Contrast the following possible reactions to a teen when he wears terrible jeans, and try to imagine how the teenager feels. Which response do you feel communicates acceptance?

Parent 1: Surely you aren't going to wear those jeans to school again! People will think we can't afford decent clothes for you. Why do you have to look that way?

Parent 2: You have been wearing those jeans a lot lately. Are they your "feel good" pants? When I see you in them I think, "that's my John!"

We have found that we are the most effective when our responses are closer to those of Parent 2. Accepting responses often pave the way for later input into the life of the young person. For example, if you can accept the worn out jeans, at some point you will be able to say, "I want to buy you some new jeans. Do you think you can wear them out so they will be 'feel good' pants too?"

Just as teenagers want to know that they can be accepted when they wear "scuzzies," they also want to try their wings at dressing up. Support without pressure seems to be the key. Teenagers know that when you tell them that they are accepted, that doesn't tell them anything. They expect that from you. What they need to know is when they are accepted by others. They also need to be shown that they are accepted by you. You may show acceptance by a smile or a pat on the knee. Often the little things mean the most.

Allow Them to Express Feelings

When your adolescent chooses to focus on his weaknesses, acceptance is not shown by trying to talk them out of it. Compare these responses.

Adolescent: I have these pimples. I must be the ugliest person alive.

Parent 1: You aren't ugly. Those pimples don't look bad at all unless you keep picking at them.

Parent 2: It's hard when you don't feel good about yourself, isn't it? I don't notice your pimples much, but I know they bother you.

In the first response the parent refuses to accept the youngster's feelings and perceptions. The lack of acceptance is further communicated by the not so subtle message to *stop picking your face.* The teenager will receive this message as further evidence of lack of acceptance. The response is often: "My parents don't even think I can take care of myself." At the risk of being redundant, I must say acceptance is communicated by identifying with your teenagers' feelings and by telling them what they are doing right. They often have an acute awareness of the things they are doing wrong.

Communicate Messages of Acceptance

What are the elements of acceptance which we as parents should strive to communicate to our teenager? Let me suggest five messages we should seek to get across to them.

1. *I enjoy you. Being with you is fun.*

Right now you might not be able to truthfully make this statement. If, however, you begin to emphasize the positive aspects of your teenagers' lives, you will find enjoyment with them. They couldn't be too bad. After all, they have decent parents.

2. *I like watching you grow. Your development is an encouragement to me.*

This statement won't ring true unless you take the time to identify your youngsters' growth points. Don't seek to give them a five point sermon on how they are growing as a person. Instead, seek to spontaneously point out evidences of their maturation as you notice them.

3. *I want to hear your ideas. They challenge me.*

Accepting your teenagers' intellectual development is a great challenge because they fluctuate between moments of pure brilliance and moments of blind, rigid naiveté. Let your teenagers' ideas challenge you. Do not try to challenge their thinking out of existence. Question their thinking, but do not tell them what to think.

4. *I like who you are becoming. I don't always know how to tell you, but you have possibilities.*

As parents, we need to find the delicate balance between acceptance of our teenagers as persons with potential and not pressuring them to be great. Our job is to keep them moving down the road—not to tell them to run faster and faster. When they decide they want to run faster we can support them, but we will only frustrate them if we try to be their source of motivation.

5. *I forgive you when you fail.*

If you want to know if you are a forgiving person, ask your teen-

agers. They will tell you. One adolescent said, "My dad may say that
he forgives, but he never lets me off the hook. He remembers everything I have ever done wrong." This type of father is what David
Seamands describes as a grievance collector.

They all owe you a debt, don't they? They owe you affection
and love, security and affirmation, but since you feel indebted
and guilty, resentful, insecure, and anxious, since you see yourself as unforgiven and unacceptable, you in turn become unfor-
giving and unaccepting. You have not received grace, so how
can you give it to others? And as you feel tormented, you hurt
others. You've got to collect on the grievances, collect on your
hurts. You must make all these people who have hurt you pay
the debts they owe you. You are a grievance collector.[3]

There is no more effective way to communicate acceptance than to
forgive the person for behavior that is unacceptable. Acceptance sepa-
rates the person from the sin. Nonacceptance demands that the person pay for the sin before he is accepted. When this structure is set up
there is no hope, because only Jesus Christ was perfect enough to pay
for sin.

3. Develop Mutual Respect

I have discovered in working with parents and children of various
ages that parents often seek to earn their children's love. This does not
work because love is not earned. Love is either given or received.
Parents also try to love their child in an almost courtship kind of way,
instead of respecting their youngsters and valuing them for who they
are.

John's dad seems to give John everything he asks for and many
things he does not even request. John feels loved but he is confused.
He feels like his dad is buying him, but he isn't able to identify what he
wants Dad to do differently. As we explored his feelings, John said, "I
feel like he is afraid to meet me man-to-man. I want him to respect me,
not buy me."

You may breathe a sigh of relief and say, "But I never try to buy my
teenagers. I don't give them things." Possibly true. But before you retreat to self-righteousness, consider ways you seek to earn love, other
than with money. One common way of trying to earn love is through
making concessions to your teenager. Letting the rules slide is a good
example. I always wonder when I hear a teenager say, "Oh, they
didn't really mean what they said." Concessions are probably being

made which will ultimately earn neither love nor respect.

Respect Their Abilities

There are three major areas of respect which need to be extended to your teenager. The first of these is *abilities.* For parents to change their perception of a teenager from a dependent to a competent person is difficult. We tend to keep our children in the cradle while they are climbing to the mountain top. When parents do not respect their youngsters' abilities, they tend to either pamper them and do everything for them, or they belittle them and create a sense of hostility.

The job of the parent is to help equip the teenager in as many areas of life as possible, and then to respect the teenagers' abilities enough to allow them to exercise those abilities on a regular basis. Too often parents treat their teenagers like slaves. They let them do the menial tasks or think the unimportant thoughts, but never really allow them to get involved in the action. Teenagers need to be respected enough to know that they have God-given abilities. They need their parents' respect so that they can go ahead and use them.

Respect Their Plans

A second important area in which teenagers need to be respected is *plans.* We live in a world where there are more opportunities than there are hours to take advantage of them. This has resulted in a heavy emphasis on planning. When you plan, it is easy to become self-centered to the point of feeling like everyone else's plans should revolve around your plans. Teenagers resent this because they themselves have to learn to be planners. They feel devalued when their plans always have to be subject to fitting into the plans of their parents.

The only way to avoid this dilemma over planning is to *wisely* plan. Ask your teenagers what plans they have and tell them what plans you have as far in advance as possible. Keeping the communication channel open will help to build mutual respect, and will also enable both you and your teenagers to get to do more of the things each of you would like to do. Teenagers feel flattered when their plans are given equal time. If you allow them this privilege, you will find them more receptive to times when you ask them to sacrifice their plans for your sake or the sake of the entire family. Working together in this way is a very valuable part of the learning process, but it requires a heavy dose of communication and working together. These are the elements out of which respect is made.

If there are events on your social calendar which you want your young people to attend, but know that they will probably not look forward to them, letting them know ahead of time is even more important. Surprises aren't fun, especially if the surprise is something you aren't sure you will enjoy. Our teenagers do not like to go to dinner at the homes of families they do not know. Visiting our friends is not always a treat for them, especially if they do not know the children of our friends. There are some times when we respect their feelings and allow them to stay home. There are also times when we demand that they go. We joke about it lightly and refer to going as "paying the family dues."

If the teenagers are allowed to express their negative feelings (hopefully in a moderate form), they will support their parents by going and occasionally they will even admit to having a good time. Planning in advance before a competing event comes up eases the tension. Putting off letting the teenager know is seen as disrespectful and will only tend to make the problem worse.

Respect Their Privacy

A third area in which the teenager needs respect is in the area of privacy. They need space in which to grow, and space in which to think their own thoughts. They need the right to have locks on their doors just as their parents do. They need to be able to leave letters and diaries out without fear of having their privacy violated. Being respected in this area helps the teenager develop self-esteem. Lack of respect of privacy by the parents results in the teenager feeling devalued or even disliked. Don't be afraid to enter your teenager's world, but do so on an invited basis.

Some parents do not have trouble respecting their teenager's physical privacy, but find it more difficult to respect their social or emotional privacy. We somehow feel that we need to know everything that is going on and everything that is being thought so that we can be the best possible parents. If this attitude becomes an obsession, you will find yourself playing cops and robbers instead of being a good parent.

Trust is more important than information in most cases. I find that I get information whether I want it or not. I usually don't accomplish anything by invading my teenager's privacy. Being available is more effective in gathering information than spying or playing twenty questions. It is difficult for parents not to worry about their teenagers because parents know most of the potential problem areas that the teenagers face. However, invasion of privacy will not allay your worries. In fact, invasion of privacy will probably make your worries worse. In the Sermon on the Mount, Jesus asked, *"Who of you by worrying can add a single hour to his life?"* (Matthew 6:27). We need to learn to respect our teenager's privacy.

4. Allow Your Teenagers to Discover Who They Are

Discovering who you are (or "finding yourself") is considered the primary need a person faces during the adolescent period. The question of "Who am I?" begins early in life, but the adolescent period is especially significant because during the adolescent years the young person begins to really see himself as a separate, unique person.

Defining One's Identity

The question "Who am I?" must be answered with positive statements. I am a man or I am a woman. I am a Christian. I am Earl and Sandy Wilson's son or daughter. I like the outdoors. I enjoy people. I dislike crowds. I enjoy laughter. I don't like to be out of control. The list of "I" statements which the teenager generates is his identity. The adolescent period is the time when these statements begin to be formulated more clearly. Parents can help the process by asking questions but not demanding answers. There is nothing more frustrating than to be seeking an answer for yourself, but not to have the answer clear in your mind before you are pressed to share it with others.

Teenagers turn to their peers because peers understand what they are going through. The wise parent will understand this and build upon it rather than be threatened by it. Don't feel that you must compete with your teenagers' friends. Keep your own identity. Your teenagers need you as a parent just as they need friends in order to understand themselves better. Get to know their friends, but do not take over their friends. You cannot engineer your child's identity foundation. You can only provide positive input and then wait for the results.

Your challenge is to trust God to use the training you have provided in a positive way during a time when the opportunity for further training has ended. If you don't have doubts regarding that training, your teenager, or yourself, you are not normal. We can always think of things we could have done differently. Remember, identity foundation is such an individualized process you cannot possibly cover all the bases. There is a point at which you must entrust your teenager to God and wait for the results.

Many Christian parents have done a better job than they realize.

The hard part is letting your training be put to the test. If you try too often to straighten a wire, your constant bending will break it. This is also true of trying to force identity development. There is a point at which the parents need to stop straightening the wire.

Identifying Elements of Maturity

How do we know when identity is achieved? What are the elements of maturity which the adolescent needs to develop? Erik Erikson spent much of his professional life seeking to answer those questions. In his biography of Erikson, Roazen abstracted Erikson's description of the mature adult as a person who:

Is tolerant of himself and those who interact with him.

Has the capacity to make informed choices.

Has the courage to stand alone.

Is able to achieve mastery in the tasks he undertakes.

Has the vision to open up new realities.

Is able to weather the conflicts he faces.

Has the capacity to do well, according to the standards of those who are significant to him.

Elaborates one of his dominant abilities (for example, his math ability) into a full-time occupation.

Is able to be childlike, and is most human when he is at play.[4]

There are two areas of identity which are not covered by Roazen's list. These are awareness of oneself as a sexual being and awareness of oneself as a spiritual being.

Identity formation is affected by the realities of life and by our perceptions of those realities. A part of the parent's role in helping to meet the identity needs of the teenager is to help him keep a positive outlook on the process of developing the elements of maturity. Growing up is difficult. Parents can help by enabling the teenager to see progress. Open, casual discussions are often the best means of accomplishing this task. A question like, "How are you feeling about your friendships?" is a helpful conversation starter. The maturing adolescent will discover himself in each area of life. Watching this discovery, although frightening, is highly satisfying for the parent who does not get scared away by the process.

5. Provide Limits in Which Your Teenager Can Function

Balanced growth by the adolescent is best encouraged by the presence of parental guidelines. Just as a plant grows the straightest when attached to a stake, so a teenager needs the stability of straight guidelines from the parents. Teenagers feel more secure when they know the boundaries of the playing field. They will disagree with the boundaries, and in some instances will ask that the boundaries be changed, but they do like boundaries.

One of the boundaries that we set for our teenagers is the rule that they must keep us informed about where they are going. We try to give them ample freedom to make decisions for themselves, but we need to know what decisions they have made. My daughter may choose to go visit a friend on a Saturday even if we are not home, but she is not free to just take off without letting us know where she has gone. This type of rule helps us to carry out our responsibilities as parents, and also forces our daughter to think about where she plans to go as she puts it down on paper. We have been pleased as we have seen her anticipate some of our concerns and allay some of our own fears by telling us why or how she has made a decision.

Limits Are Based on Relationship and Authority

Guidelines are not shackles to prevent growth. They are aids to growth. I believe that successful setting of limits for the teenager is based on two important variables: relationship and authority. To successfully set limits for my teenagers, I must first strengthen my relationship with them. I best provide guidelines when I know my teenager. I must be willing to pay the price in order to earn the right to be heard.

The second aspect of setting limits is authority. Our teenagers know that we are not always right, but we are the parents. We set limits because we are their parents. We allow them to express themselves, but we also expect them to respect us both as parental authorities and as individual people. My father never allowed me to speak disrespectfully to my mother. That was an important limit which helped mold my growth. I accepted that authority more readily because of the relationship which we had. The two go together.

Discuss reasonable limits for growth with your teenagers. They will respect and value most of those decisions which they get to help make. Limits can be set which meet the needs of the teenager as well as the parents' needs. Once again, open discussion and sharing of your perception of needs can be invaluable in arriving at limits which will meet both sets of needs.

Delegating Authority to Set Limits

Transferring the limiting process from the authority of the parent to the teenager is important. Adolescents need to learn to set limits for themselves. "What kind of limits do you need to put on yourself to help you reach your goals?" is a helpful question to ask your teens. Unfortunately, many teenagers get to the point of leaving home without ever learning to set limits for themselves. This is inadequate training. Healthy self-control requires experience in thinking through various possibilities, considering options, and then setting the limits that are useful in reaching goals.

A teenager cannot learn to set limits for himself unless he has observed his parents' use of limits and has also been given the responsibility for limiting himself. When Jesus spoke about being a disciple, He emphasized carrying our cross (which could be viewed as setting limits on ourselves) and counting the cost (which is another aspect of limit setting). Notice how these two fit together in Luke 14:27-30.

> *"And anyone who does not carry his cross and follow me cannot be my disciple. Suppose one of you wants to build a tower. Will he not first sit down and estimate the cost to see if he has enough money to complete it? For if he lays the foundation and is not able to finish it, everyone who sees it will ridicule him, saying, 'This fellow began to build and was not able to finish.'"*

Balancing Relationship and Authority

In considering limit setting, it is important to remember that there must be a balance established with relationship and authority. This balance is presented in Figure 3.

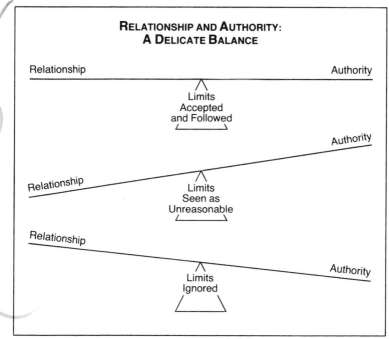

Figure 3

When the relationship is low, the limits will be seen as arbitrary or unfair and will often not be respected. When the authority is too low, the limits will be ignored or not respected and the teenagers will become a law unto themselves. The adolescent needs limits for healthy growth. The role of the parent is to provide the balance of relationship and authority so that the limits are effective.

6. Allow Your Teenager to Experience the Consequences of His Behavior

Experiencing the consequences of their behavior doesn't seem like a need of teenagers at first glance. But after careful consideration, most teenagers admit that they learn best when they have to face up to their own behavior. Parents have a tendency to err on one side or the other. Either we *overprotect* our children and do not allow them to experience the consequences of their behavior or we *underprotect* them and do not prepare them for certain consequences which they might expect. There is a third error that we commit, which is to *punish* inappropriate behavior when teenagers need to learn the natural consequences of inappropriate behavior. Let's look at each of these three errors.

Overprotection

Why is overprotection ineffective in meeting your teenagers' needs? When I overprotect my teenagers, I teach them that behavior does not have consequences. They come to believe that they can do anything they want to do and it won't make any difference. If they ever do get completely on their own after being overprotected, they are in for a rude awakening. They will suddenly realize that the world has teeth. Learning this gradually as a part of the normal growth process is much easier for the teenager.

Underprotection

Underprotection creates a different kind of problem. All of us like to know what we are in for and become resentful if we are constantly put into new circumstances without adequate preparation. Consider for a moment how you might answer an adolescent who asks what high school is like. He needs to be prepared for some of the hazing that freshmen often receive. He needs to be oriented to the different standards held by teachers and the way certain rules are enforced. In some instances sharing ideas about what to expect prepares the adolescent to take more control of his own life. But you cannot protect them from failure. And you cannot predict the unknown. You can only share the information that you have and leave the response up to the teenager.

Punishment

The error of punishing rather than letting the teenager experience the consequences of his behavior is important to elaborate. Punishment is not always connected to behavior in the mind of the adolescent. Punishment is often viewed as arbitrary and unjust if this connection is not made. This is one of the reasons why punishment is sometimes ineffective. Punishment is most effective when it is directly related to the undesirable behavior. The effect of punishment is weakened by combining punishment with encouragement of the desired behaviors. Another problem with punishment is the delay between the offense and the delivery of the punishment. If the delay is long, the effect will be lost.

In contrast, the consequences of a particular behavior are usually felt tragically if the parent doesn't intervene. If your adolescent goofs around and misses the school bus, the natural consequence would be to let him walk home. This would be more effective than grounding him or verbally punishing him. We tend to use unrelated punishment because we are fearful about his safety or possibly for some other good reasons. My point is we can become so concerned that we never let the young person live with the results of his behavior. Common sense needs to be carefully blended with an awareness of the needs of teenagers to learn what the real world is like.

Searching for Your Teenager's Unique Needs

Any discussion of the needs of adolescents would be incomplete without the reminder that your adolescent is unique. He has needs which you, as a parent, or I, as a professional psychologist, cannot anticipate. In fact, your teenager may not know his own unique needs. As a parent, you need to be open to being shown by God just what your special person needs as you talk with him, observe him, and pray for him. You may see areas where you can relate in new ways that will give your teenager a new sense of completeness. The key is discovery. You are searching for what is there, not creating a need on his behalf. All teenagers and all parents have numerous needs. God's intention is that some of these needs be met through our mutual interaction. Realizing that intention is exciting.

Footnotes

[1]H. A. Murray and others, *Explorations in Personality* (New York: Oxford Press, 1938), pp. 123-24.
[2]John Powell, *Unconditional Love* (Niles, Ill.: Argus Communications, 1978), pp. 66, 68.
[3]David A. Seamands, *Healing for Damaged Emotions* (Wheaton, Ill.: Victor Books, 1981), p. 33.
[4]P. Roazen, *Erik H. Erikson* (New York: Free Press, 1976), pp. 65-66.

Chapter 5

Identifying the Tasks of Parenting Teens

I'll try, Lord, but I don't know what to do.

Parenting, like marriage, is a job that most people enter into with little or no training. We somehow feel that we know how to perform these important functions automatically. Because this attitude exists, parents are often unwilling to admit that they are ill prepared. We just stumble on blindly, hoping that everything will turn out okay and that no one will notice our blunders.

One of the reasons the teen years are so devastating for many parents is that the patterns that worked during the child's early years suddenly don't work anymore. This causes panic and guilt for parents who believe they should be able to handle any situation. I believe that parents are able to handle situations successfully with their teenagers if they know what they are supposed to handle. What are the tasks that parents should seek to accomplish?

In this chapter we will survey seven of the tasks that parents have in parenting teens. The list is not intended to be exhaustive, but it is helpful for giving parents a sense of direction. Each of the seven areas is complex; therefore, the final chapters of the book will elaborate each area in more detail. Our purpose here is to orient you to your role as a parent of teenagers, and to whet your appetite for the pleasures of the job once you understand what you are doing.

Your Main Job Is to Work Yourself
out of a Job

Many criticize modern manufacturing because of what is called "planned obsolescence." That is, products are designed to be useful for only a short time, and then a new product is introduced to take its place. Many products are cheaply made because they are not intended to last.

We may despise this aspect of our throw-away society, but the concept of planned obsolescence is a valuable concept when you are viewing your role as a parent. Your major task is to work yourself out of a job. In other words, you are to help your children not to need your help any longer. This is a difficult concept for parents to grasp because they have a strong desire to feel needed. This is why God intended that our needs be met within our roles as husband and wife, and not met primarily by our children.

In the late 1970s, when the so-called "no-fault divorce" laws were instituted, literally thousands of couples divorced who had been married more than twenty years. I believe that one of the reasons this happened was that husbands and wives were living for their children and not for each other. If your needs are being met by your children and not your spouse, the home becomes a place of cold isolation rather than continued warmth when the children leave. The Bible makes this quite clear: *"For this reason a man will leave his father and mother and be united to his wife, and they will become one flesh"* (Genesis 2:24).

The role of the parents is to continue to cleave to each other while preparing their children to leave and cleave to someone else. When this does not take place, the result is a propagation of dysfunctional families and unhappy individuals.

Identifying the Seven Tasks
of Parenting Teenagers

The parenting tasks which are identified below highlight three important functions which we are to fulfill with our teenagers. These are the development of social skills, education, and the development of ego strength. *Communication,* which is a social skill task, is discussed first because it is the platform from which the other functions are accomplished.

Next, two aspects of education are considered: *spiritual education* and *moral development.* These are areas in which parents need to play a vital role. For the Christian parent, this education is the payoff. Other people may teach my children reading, writing, and arithmetic, but if I am to *"train a child in the way he should go"* (Proverbs 22:6), I must also be involved in the important area of character development.

Three ego development tasks are elaborated. These ego tasks include helping the child *to become autonomous or self-sufficient, to develop self-acceptance,* and *to accept responsibility.* Acceptance of responsibility is considered only a social skill by some, but I have put it in the ego development category. Teenagers need to see themselves as being responsible persons. As one becomes responsible, one is normally also seen as being more skilled socially.

The second aspect of social skills discussed is *friendship.* The emphasis in Chapter 12 is on the friendship between parent and teenager. In this chapter we will introduce some of the same principles, but will apply them to the general process of developing friendships. Let's get an overview now of the seven tasks of parenting teens.

Task #1: Communication: The Key to Parenting Teens

Recently I called my home: The telephone rang twice and then was silent. I said, "Hello," once just to see what would happen: nothing. I waited for a short time and then hung up the receiver and started the whole process over again.

After one ring I was greeted by the cheery voice of my wife. "Was that you who just called?" she asked. "I was just talking up a storm when I realized you weren't there any longer. I heard you say, 'Hello,' and then you didn't talk to me anymore." At that point we each realized the problem. She could hear me but I couldn't hear her. We had to start over in order to get both lines of communication open. It didn't do any good for her to talk if I wasn't hearing. We were both just getting frustrated.

This incident illustrates so well what happens between parents and teens. Both may be trying to communicate, but the system isn't working. One is talking but the other isn't hearing. One is listening but the other doesn't seem to speak. There is a need to hang up and start all over. Unfortunately, in parent-teen relationships the system malfunctions frequently and the receiver is often left dangling in silence. When this happens, decisions are made on hunches rather than on facts. Misunderstandings deepen and relationships begin to deteriorate.

The Process of Communicating

Effective parent-teen communication requires a clear cut awareness of what is involved in the communication process. First and foremost, communication is an exchange . . . an exchange of ideas, feelings, plans, expectations, and values. When you communicate with someone, you get to know them, and you allow them to get to know you at the same level.

Sending a message does little or no good if it isn't received by someone. Likewise, sending a message and never knowing how it was received by the person to whom it was sent is very frustrating. The following diagram illustrates the total exchange process.

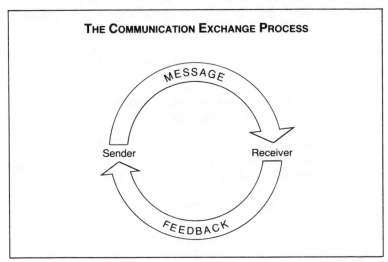

THE COMMUNICATION EXCHANGE PROCESS

MESSAGE

Sender

Receiver

FEEDBACK

Figure 4

In normal communication the sender and receiver roles will alternate between the two people. If good communication is to take place, however, each exchange must be complete. The feedback loop, interacting with the communication that was sent, provides this completion of the exchange.

Tips for More Effective Communication

Specifying exactly what you would like to accomplish as you seek to communicate with your teenager is helpful. The following list suggests some ideas for improving parent-teen communication.

   1. Try to be receptive to any message that your teenager

sends.

2. Try to understand the message rather than correct it.

3. Verbally paraphrase the message back to your teenager to make sure you received it without distorting it.

4. Send messages that will help the teenager to get to know you better.

5. Don't assume that you know what the other person is thinking. Not even psychologists are mind readers.

6. Send messages to keep your teenager informed about your plans. Surprises create resentment.

7. Enjoy the process. Don't get so task-oriented that you become uptight. Relax!

In any process there are certain precautions which need to be taken in order to insure success. The suggestions compiled by John Dacey are helpful.

- Always keep your lines of communication open.
- You should listen more than you talk. Try to give each kid time to think of and express his feelings.
- Be aware that each kid is an individual and has his own individual way of expressing things.
- Be a good listener. Many of these children have no one else that they trust and who will listen to them.
- Never betray confidentiality. Trust is vital to everything you do with them.
- Don't always expect to get positive feedback from them.
- Always avoid using diagnostic labels. These labels tend to turn into self-fulfilling prophecies.
- Never accept a confidence which you cannot honestly keep. [1]

As you focus on opening up communication with your teenagers, you will sooner or later hear some of the most beautiful words ever spoken: "I really enjoyed talking to you."

Task #2: Pass on Your Faith

There are many things that parents pass on to their children whether they want to or not. Physical appearance, temperament, habits, and family reputation are some of the most obvious. We enjoy knowing that our children are chips off the old block. Even teenagers secretly enjoy this fact, although they sometimes wish they had inherited something less than a size EEE nose. They want their own identity, but they also want to be proud of their roots. I still get goose bumps at times when I realize that I am Claude and Emma Wilson's son. Neither were famous. They both led modest lives. But to me they were wonderful, powerful people. They passed on life, Christian faith, and many healthy examples about how to live both.

What about the things that aren't passed along automatically? There are areas where transmission between generations requires planning and diligence. Passing along your faith is such a process. It requires planning and diligence. Passing on your faith is difficult because faith is a personal matter that requires personal choices and involvement. These matters can be influenced but not legislated. You can't make anyone believe. You can only seek to help them understand why belief in God is reasonable for you and why it should be carefully considered by them. The more you are able to talk about your personal faith without pressuring your teenager to blindly conform, the greater the possibility will be of passing it on to your teen.

I believe the most important element in passing on your faith is communicating the "gospel." "Gospel" means "good news." The possibility of a personal relationship with God is good news! The gospel needs to be communicated with joy. I was attracted to the faith of my mother because it put a smile on her face. I knew that her faith was a real part of her pleasant personality. She was less uptight than most people because she was living with a greater purpose than being nit-picky. I watched as she lived the faith before my dad, an unbeliever. I saw her love him more than she loved the idea of his being a Christian.

I remember vividly a time when we attended evangelistic meetings at our church. Dad went! The altar call was given and the enthusiastic leader lied. He said there would be only one more verse of the final song, but he asked us to sing another, and another, and another. I was impressed when I heard Mom whisper into Dad's ear, "If he sings one more verse I'm walking out. Do you want to go with me?" She knew Dad's salvation was in God's hands, not hers. Fifteen years later it happened.

Neither Mom nor Dad ever used God as a threat. They presented Him and lived their lives with Him as an opportunity. That's the approach to faith they passed on, and that's the faith I am endeavoring to pass on to my children—a deep respect for God and a capacity to enjoy Him. As parents, we need to evaluate what we are trying to do. Many teenagers leave home with the picture that God is one who zaps you when you get out of line, period. This distorted view of God thwarts, rather than fosters, spiritual development. Be positive! Be open. And apply the principles of faith you want to teach as you relate with your teenager, as is discussed in Chapter 7.

Task #3: Share Your Values

In recent years we have seen the birth of such social movements as the "New Morality" on one hand, and (more recently) the "Moral Majority" on the other. Both of these movements represent strong attempts to affect the moral and value structure of our youth. All social movements try to tell people what to believe and how to behave. Some parents have been intimidated by these movements, particularly when their children have listened to the propaganda and have then tried to tell their parents that their values are old-fashioned or inadequate for a modern world.

One parent lamented, "How can I compete? They don't seem to care what I believe." Wrong! Teenagers do care what you believe, and they care deeply. They just aren't going to swallow it whole without chewing it and tasting it for awhile. They want you to share your values with them because your value system is the only value system they are able to scrutinize in depth. They observe what others believe and how they live, but not at the same depth that they look at the life you have chosen. One of the big educational tasks of parents is to share their values.

Albert Bandura and his colleagues at Stanford University have clearly shown that human modeling has one of the greatest effects upon the learning of values and attitudes by persons of all ages. Conclusions from their research are described below.

> One of the most dependable sets of events that has been found to produce changes in attitudes is the phenomenon of human modeling. In these circumstances, learning results in imitation of action choices. When suitable designed learning conditions are present, the learner acquires an attitude which reflects that expressed or demonstrated by the human model.[2]

Modeling of values and moral behavior takes place when a respected person, like a parent, is observed acting in a certain way in a certain situation. The observer sees what values the parent claims to have and, more importantly, sees what values are lived out. The teenager who is observing then sees the results of the behavior. If the results seem positive, then the teenager will at least try to imitate the values or moral behavior of the parent.

My dad believed that honesty is the best policy, for example. I didn't learn to be honest, however, by hearing this phrase. Dad modeled honesty for me. I remember watching carefully when I knew Dad received too much change from the sales clerk. He gave it back. She thanked him, smiled, told him how much she appreciated an honest man. As we walked out of the store, I could see the satisfaction on Dad's face. His modeling of honesty taught me to be honest in this kind of situation as well as to maintain honesty as a life principle.

Modeling values is an important task of parenting teenagers. If modeling is consistently carried out, the teenager will be much more apt to come to the parent to seek consultation related to values. This consistent role is what I believe the parent should seek. Some possible ways of achieving this goal are discussed in Chapter 8.

Task #4: Encourage Autonomy

Parents of adolescents are caught in an interesting bind. We would like to be free from the hassles and responsibilities of parenting, but at the same time we are afraid to turn loose. We fear that we will find out that we have not done all that we were supposed to do. We fluctuate between feeling totally worthless (wishing we could quit), and feeling totally responsible (wanting to do everything for our teenagers).

In our more rational moments we recognize the need to produce offspring who can stand on their own two feet. We don't want them to remain dependent and yet a part of our own sense of worth is to know that others are dependent on us. The dangers are clear. If we are not careful, we will create a situation where our teenagers are dependent on us in ways that are not healthy for us in the long run, and that prevent them from developing the autonomy they need to take their productive places in society.

What does encouraging autonomy mean? Autonomy means being independent from the direct assistance or uninvited input of the parent. I can be autonomous and still want my dad's advice. I am not autonomous if I cannot ask him for advice because I will have to do what he says. I am also not autonomous if I cannot act without asking for his advice. Encourage your teenagers to seek advice, but also help them to realize that the decisions are theirs, and that you believe they are able to make good decisions. This process is aptly described by Ginott.

A wise parent makes himself increasingly dispensable to his teenagers. He sympathetically watches the drama of growth, but resists the desire to intervene too often. Out of concern and respect, whenever possible, he allows his teenagers to make their own choices and to use their own powers. His language is deliberately sprinkled with statements that encourage independence:

The choice is yours.

You decide about that.

If you want to.

It's your decision.

Whatever you choose is fine with me.[3]

One question to ask yourself is, "Am I doing for my teenagers what they probably should be doing for themselves?" Freedom from *doing for* your teenager gives you the time to *do with* them, or to provide them with special assistance when they, like you and me, get in over their heads. Such help at that point will be seen as an act of love, whereas too much *doing for* them is viewed as your refusal to allow them to grow up. *Doing with* results in an opportunity to grow closer, as well as an opportunity for the teenager to learn from you. *Doing for* usually doesn't accomplish anything.

True autonomy is achieved when the teenager develops a sense of self-respect accompanied by a responsible spirit and a willingness to reach and set goals. Five steps for equipping your teens to achieve autonomy are discussed in Chapter 9.

Task #5: Nurture Self-Acceptance

The choice of the word "nurture" in relationship to "self-acceptance" is deliberate. Self-acceptance on the part of the adolescent requires careful nurturance on the part of the parents. The human spirit is like a tender plant that needs food, water, and lots of sunshine. Webster defines "nurturance" as "affectionate care and attention."[4]

As a parent, I need to first attend to my teenagers' conditions to nurture their self-acceptance. I cannot assume that just because *I* feel good about them, *they* will feel good about themselves. I criticize my teenagers and move beyond that to a place of accepting them despite their imperfections. But they get hung up on my criticism, however, and develop feelings of guilt or self-hatred because of their belief that they need to keep me happy at all times. In other words, their standards are often higher than mine. I need to pay attention to that.

The notion of "affectionate care" is also related to self-acceptance. Affection is the soil in which self-acceptance is most likely to grow. Loving is much easier for me when I know others love me. Believing that God loves me, which is the foundation for true self-acceptance, is easier when I know that others love me. The importance to self-acceptance of feeling loved cannot be overstated. Narramore explains this well.

The final ingredient in our self-concept is the feeling of being loved. Probably the best-known verse in the New Testament is John 3:16, which reads, "For God so loved the world that He gave His one and only Son, that whoever believes in Him shall not perish but have everlasting life." Here, in a nutshell, is the best foundation for a lasting attitude of self-love. Even before we were born, God chose us to be His children. The Apostle Paul writes, "For He chose us in Him before the creation of the world to be holy and blameless in His sight. In love He predestined us to be adopted as sons through Jesus Christ, in accordance with His pleasure and will" (Eph. 1:4-5).[5]

In addition to providing loving support, I believe the greatest way to help your teenagers with self-acceptance is to help them tell the truth about themselves. They do not need to be overly humble to be worthwhile, nor do they need to be the greatest to be accepted. All of us need to learn to tell the truth about ourselves. This notion is expanded in Chapter 10, but suffice it to say at this point that the self-accepting teenager has a grasp of both his strengths and weaknesses.

A self-accepting person says, "I am average," and knows that to be average means that perhaps half of the people are better, but half are also not as good. A person with poor self-acceptance says, "I'm average," but means, "I'm in the lowest group." This person doesn't allow the reality of his abilities to penetrate into his awareness. He needs help in realism. He needs to tell it like it is. Sometimes children have been led to believe that there is virtue in degrading one's self. As you will see in Chapter 10, I do not see self-degradation as consistent with a biblically based view of self.

In her book, *Peoplemaking*, Virginia Satir underscores the need for nurturance within the family.

Perhaps one of the distinguishing features of nurturing parents is that they realize that change is inevitable: Children change quickly from one state to another, nurturing adults never stop growing and changing; and the world around us never stands still. They accept change as an unavoidable part of being alive and try to use it creatively to make their families still more nurturing.[6]

Asking teenagers to tell the truth about themselves is nurturing because this forces them to go beyond the clichés or derogatory statements behind which they hide, and to really evaluate themselves and what God is doing in their young lives. Telling the truth is hard, but a healthy activity.

Task #6: Develop Responsibility

Take a moment and ask yourself a simple but profound question: *How and when did I become responsible?* If you don't like that question, here is another: *What conditions enabled me to reach the level of responsibility in which I find myself?*

Regardless of how we ourselves have learned responsibility, we tend to treat our children as though we believe that they will only become responsible if we tell them enough times how things are to be done. This was brought home forcefully to my attention recently when we had an ice storm in Portland. I listened to both Sandy and me try to help our daughter become a responsible winter driver. Daily each of us told her how to stop, how to go, how careful to be. We each stressed the need to let the car do the work without using too much gas.

The first time she was able to try her skills, she used too much gas and barely got out of the driveway. It was clear to us that there was no direct relationship between our lectures and her level of responsibility. She made it to school and back safely, and in the process began to learn for herself how important controlling the amount of gas is when you are trying to get moving on the ice.

I am not suggesting that warning and instructing are unimportant; however, I would have been a delinquent parent if I had not been conscious of the fact that my daughter was not prepared. What I realized, however, is that piling one warning upon another doesn't really help the teenager gain responsibility. Warning is not a substitute for experience. I sometimes think that when young people are told something more than once, they get the idea that it is too difficult for them to learn from their parents, and so they focus on learning by their own trial and error. This may be deflating to my parental ego, but I was thankful that my daughter did become responsible despite my incessant warnings, which only served to close her ears.

Another important aspect in helping teenagers develop responsibility is allowing them to assess their own situation without overemphasizing their mistakes. Asking them to consider what outcome they would have liked is much more effective than telling them how they failed. They already know how they failed. That doesn't need to be underscored.

When your son comes home late because he lost track of the time, harshly rebuking him doesn't help him become responsible. What helps is to ask him to think of some ways he might be able to keep better track of the time. You will find that he wants to be successful, and that he will deeply appreciate your assistance, especially when he expected only punishment. When your teens are responsible, tell them how much you enjoy watching this aspect of their development. But don't tell them in front of their friends. That will only embarrass them. Tell them in private, or make a joke of it if you do it in front of their brothers and sisters. I asked my son at the dinner table, "What am I going to do with you? You are becoming responsible, and I'm losing all my excuses for worrying and acting critically." He grinned and I knew that he received the message.

In some instances writing messages of encouragement is helpful. In the quietness and privacy of his room your teenager will read the message and grow to new levels of responsible behavior. These are just a few of the many ways to encourage your teenager to develop responsibility. Chapter 11 discusses this area in much more detail.

Task #7: Help Your Child to Become a Friend

The final task of parenting to be discussed is the task of teaching your child how to be a friend. This important task is often overlooked because we, as parents, either don't know how to be friends ourselves, or we assume that being a friend is something that everyone learns automatically. If friendship skills came automatically, fewer people would be without friends. The truth is that most teenagers, like their parents, are woefully inadequate in this area.

In discussing the process of friendship, James and Savary have described six stages.

> The choices people make of whether or not to be friends and whether or not to become close friends seem to follow a certain process. . . . The first state is meeting in a *matrix* for friendship. Next in the process, people greet each other and get *acquainted.* They discover a sense of *"we-ness."* Out of this, a *casual friendship* begins to form. Building a *close friendship* is the next step and eventually, a *third self* of friendship may develop.[7]

Without taking time to discuss the various stages of the process, I must point out that parents need to observe where their teenager is in the process. Some teenagers refuse to enter the matrix where friendships are formed. They are usually afraid of rejection. Others are not able to go beyond the acquaintanceship phase. They need help in knowing how to go deeper.

As a parent, you cannot force friendships, but you may provide the environment in which friendship can happen. Do not be afraid to have teenagers around your house. Provide fun things for them to do. Do not tell your child whom to select for a friend. This will only put additional pressure on them to conform to your expectations, rather than to evaluate their own needs for friendship, and to seek out the type of person they need.

I do believe in asking teenagers to evaluate their friendships, however. One way to do that is to ask them what kind of friends they want and who the prospects are. In doing this you discover where you can help. For example, if they tell you the type of person they want for a friend and who is like that, encourage them to invite one or more of these people to accompany your family for a picnic or a short trip. These experiences will give your adolescents an opportunity to learn about their own capacity for friendship.

Be helpful by providing a listening ear when your teenagers experience breakdowns in friendships. Don't try to fix things for them, but do listen and identify with their hurts. When you have listened, give them some ideas to try if they want to resume the relationship. If they try one of them and find that it works, they will think you are both beautiful and brilliant. They will also value their friendship with you even more.

The final chapter of this volume is devoted to the specific friendship between a parent and teenager. It contains a number of principles to teach your teenagers in order to help them develop friendship skills. There is no substitute for doing, and if they learn friendship from you they will be able to use these friendship skills with others.

Setting the Focus

In taking a final look at the tasks of parenting, it is helpful to realize that this job is our most important responsibility. Your job is helping people we love to become all that they can become. We have the opportunity to turn the tide in a positive direction for our teenagers.

Footnotes

[1]John Steward Dacey, *Adolescents Today* (Santa Monica: Goodyear Publishing Co., Inc., 1979), p. 397.

[2]Robert M. Gagné, *The Conditions of Learning,* 3d ed. (New York: Holt, Rinehart and Winston, 1977), p. 245.

[3]Haim G. Ginott, *Between Parent and Teenager* (New York: Avon Books, 1969), p. 37.

[4]*Webster's New Collegiate Dictionary,* 1979 ed., s.v. "nurturance."

[5]S. Bruce Narramore, *You're Someone Special* (Grand Rapids, Mich.: Zondervan Publishing House, 1978), p. 132.

[6]Virginia Satir, *Peoplemaking* (Palo Alto: Science and Behavior Books, Inc., 1972), pp. 17-18.

[7]Muriel James and Louis Savary, *The Heart of Friendship* (New York: Harper and Row, 1978), p. 34.

Chapter 6

Establishing and Maintaining Communication

I try to talk to him, Lord,
but he just won't listen.

One of the most common complaints of parents regarding their children is, "He just won't listen to me." With tears in her eyes, a mother prayed, "I try to talk to him, Lord, but he just won't listen." If you talk to teens, on the other hand, they say their parents "just don't listen." That a parent (or parents) and a teenager can live under the same roof, each wanting to be in contact with the other and neither feeling the other is willing, is amazing. This tragedy has resulted in more heartache than anything else—except the heartache created by man's refusal to listen to God.

What is communication? Why is it so difficult? Webster includes the following in the definition of "communicate": "share . . . to make known . . . to reveal by clear signs . . . to transmit information, thought, or feeling so that it is satisfactorily received or understood."[1] The analogy of two rooms is useful to speak about communication: The door must be opened so that there is unimpeded passage between each room. When the door is closed, it is impossible to transmit information or share feelings.

The concern of both parents and teenagers that neither listens suggests that information, thought, and feelings are not transmitted in such a way that they are satisfactorily received or understood. Sharing is not taking place. The signs are not clear. Doors are not being opened.

Power struggles between the adolescent and the parent develop around these areas of communication. Each blames the other for the

85

lack of communication, and neither is willing to meet near the middle. If you want to improve your ability to communicate with your adolescent, I strongly suggest that you develop the attitude that it all depends on you. You need communication, and you need to take the responsibility for changing so that it will happen. If you wait for the other person to change, you will wait too long. When I talk to teens, I say exactly the same thing—"the burden of change is on you. You cannot change your parents." Obviously the process is much smoother if both people are willing to learn, but you have to begin some place, and that place is with you.

Sandy and our son, Mike, sat down together to try to talk through a conflict they were having. As they talked, each identified changes which needed to be made. They each said, "I'll try to change," and went on their way. Sandy told me how pleased she was with Mike's change. As we drove to town together I told him what his mother had said. His smile showed me how happy he was. "By the way," I said, "How is Mom doing?" "Oh, she's doing good! We're both doing good!" he replied. The door between them was unlocked and swinging open.

Communication Is More Than Talking

If you ask 100 people to define "communication" using only one word, the most common answer you will hear is "talk." You cannot have good communication without talking. However, much talking takes place with no communication occurring.

As a child, I remember being fascinated as I listened to my Dad's brother and sister argue. No matter what the issue was, they would take different sides and each would talk as fast as possible without totally cutting off the other person. As I listened one day I realized that they had completely changed sides of the issue and neither seemed to know or care. They were heavily into talking but not into communicating.

Talking only results in communication when there is a listener, just as a transmitter only produces a radio broadcast when there is a receiver. In trying to communicate with my teenagers, I sometimes become painfully aware of my tendency to talk too much and to listen too little. Let me share with you what I consider to be the acid test. If your child has normal hearing and you find that you have to repeat anything to them more than three times, you are talking too much. Either you are taking too much responsibility for them or you are telling them things they already know.

A mother related to me that she was warning her daughter several times a day about what might happen if she didn't start doing her homework. She just couldn't understand why the daughter wasn't changing. I asked her if the child was either retarded or deaf. "No!" she replied, almost horrified at the thought. "Then, let's assume that you are wasting your time and hurting the relationship because you are telling her things she already knows. Why not invest your energies in trying to help her discover why she can't act on what she knows?" Repeating clichés or preaching isn't helpful at this point.

Communication Involves Active Listening

If talking is not communication, then what is communication? Listening isn't all there is to communicating, but it really helps. A good way to evaluate your communication skills is to have someone keep track of the amount of time you talk, and the amount of time you listen, as you interact with one of your teenagers. If you talk more than you listen, try to reverse this pattern. If you have more than one conversation with your teenagers in which you talk less than half the time, they will notice the change. One sixteen-year-old said to a friend, "I don't know what's wrong with my parents. They've started to listen! I hope it's not a trap."

Keeping track of the number of times you change the subject is another way to evaluate your listening skills. When you are changing the subject often, you are only listening to respond—not to hear what the other person is saying. Consider how devastating this is to communication by remembering your last conversation with someone who repeatedly did this to you. Instead of changing the subject with your teenagers, ask them to tell you more about the current subject. They will love it and so will you. By listening you will discover that some of the things your children say which seem boring to you, become exciting as you learn more about them.

Communication experts have made a distinction between active and passive listening. Passive listening tries to hear the words, but doesn't get into the story. Active listening shares the experience, becoming involved to the point of living the experience with the other person. Active listening usually involves attending to both the context of what is being said and the feelings behind that context. Statements like: "How did you feel right then? Were you afraid? How did you keep from losing control of the car?" are examples of active listening. Active listening asks. It doesn't tell. Consider the difference in the two simulated conversations below.

Joe: Dad, you wouldn't believe what happened to me today.

Dad: Oh really?

Joe: Yeah. I had a close call.

Dad: Are you all right?

Joe: Yeah, just a little shook.

Dad: That's good. We better eat now.

Joe walks away scratching his head. He doesn't understand what happened. Anger wells within him when he realizes he didn't even have a chance to tell his story. Notice the contrast in the following interaction.

Joe: Dad, you wouldn't believe what happened to me today.

Dad: Oh, really! Tell me about it.

Joe: I had a very close call.

Dad: (Pause).

Joe continues: A lady ran a stop sign at the bottom of the hill by the school and my friends and I almost met our Maker.

Dad: Did you get hit?

Joe: No, she missed us, but boy, was it close. I'm still shaking.

Dad: I'm glad you are okay, Son (pause).

Joe: Dad, I was really scared! My friends could have been killed.

Although this example is simulated, it is true to life. When parents listen, ask questions, and stay with the adolescent, the intimacy implied by Joe sharing his deep fears often happens. This outcome is desirable for both the parent and the teenager.

The Goal of Communication is Understanding

The communication model presented in Figure 5 shows the ultimate goal of communication: to understand the other person and to be understood by him.

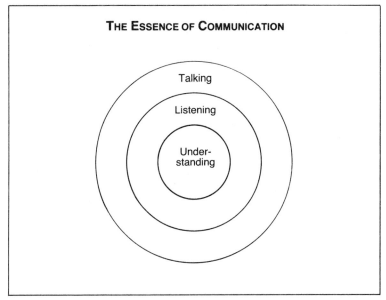

Figure 5

You will note that understanding is the core or heart of communication. When you understand someone, you hear not only the words they say, but also the music which accompanies those words. "Mom's really with it today," Ginny said. "She knew what I was feeling before I got the words out." Ginny's mom communicated understanding by her attentiveness and patient listening, not by interrupting Ginny to tell her that she understood. When you are understood by someone you know, they don't have to tell you. Be careful not to imply that people are so simple that they are easily understood.

I once overheard two of my teenagers talking. After several minutes the younger said, "I know what you mean. I got it." Quizzically, the older said, "You do? It still doesn't make much sense to me."

If you want to understand and show empathy, do not listen just for facts. Listen for the meaning that those facts have for your teenager. Listen for confusion, but allow the person to work through that confusion for himself. Listen for emotion, but do not be intimidated by what you hear.

One of my greatest discoveries as a father was to realize that I could try to understand my daughter's emotional turmoil without feeling that I had to fix it for her. I was amazed to learn that she felt I had been helpful, although as far as I could tell I hadn't done a thing except keep my ears open and my mouth shut. She was able to return to calmness just by knowing that I was there, with her, seeking to understand.

Tournier has pointed out that two main reasons people don't open up to each other are fear of being misunderstood and fear of being given advice. Your communication with your teens will be improved as you listen to understand and avoid giving advice.

Teenagers try to communicate their feelings to us in very indirect ways. My son has a hard time saying, "I'm afraid," but as I listen to him and watch his reactions I sometimes get the message. Sometimes when I try to check it out with him he says, "I'm not exactly afraid, just nervous, I guess. I don't know what to do." When you hear a statement such as this, resist the temptation to tell him what to do. True understanding will be communicated by asking, "What would you like to see happen?" or "Are you wanting help or just wanting me to know?" Either of these responses avoids the trap of giving advice and then becoming angry when the advice is not followed.

Learn to Find the Safe Pad

Imagine you are called into a courtroom before a judge and told everything you have done wrong. Would you feel close to the judge? Of course not. If the judge happened to be your friend, however, and if he invited you to have lunch to discuss one minor infraction, you would be much more open and more capable of hearing what he had to share. Better still, if you are good at playing golf and you met your friend on the course, you would probably be even more relaxed. In a sense, the golf course is your safe pad. You feel most comfortable there.

Let's consider how this concept relates to parent-teen relationships. Many young people feel very uncomfortable in the adult world of their parents. They don't know whether or not they fit. Unfortunately, when parents want to communicate with their children, they invite their children into the safe pad of their adult world. The adolescent responds by being nervous and uneasy. This upsets parents, and a power struggle ensues. "Why can't he just relax?" Dad asks himself from the comfort of his favorite chair in his den. In the meantime, son John is saying to himself, "It's always so quiet in here. I never hear Dad laugh. He's probably going to give it to me again." Is it any wonder that John and Dad have trouble communicating?

Earlier I stated that if you want to communicate with someone, you have to assume the responsibility for making the changes that are necessary for communication to occur. Let's consider the positive outcome that would occur if Dad is willing to enter John's safe pad instead of demanding that John come to his place of security.

Dad feels a need to talk with John so he looks for him. (Notice the use of the preposition "with" instead of "at," "to," or worse yet, "down to.") Dad finds John in his room and knocks on the door. He wonders if the knock can be heard above the radio. John yells, "Come in," but stays on his bed. There he lies propped up with a book, reading while the radio is blasting. Dad resists the temptation to yell, "How can you study with all that racket?" Calling it noise would be an understatement, he chuckles to himself.

Dad: John, can we talk for a minute.

John: Sure, dad. What's on your mind?

Dad: I've been feeling like there is a lot of distance between us lately and I want to know what you think.

John: (He lays down his book.) What do you mean, Dad?

Dad: I feel like we may be avoiding each other and I don't want that. I don't want it to become hard for you to talk to me.

John: I'm okay with where things are. I'm just. . . . (John moves to turn the radio down. Dad's faith in a God who cares is strengthened.) I've had so much homework I feel swamped. I haven't been avoiding you on purpose.

Dad: That feels better. I know I've been hard to catch as well. What about going out to bowl a line or two as soon as you are through with your tests?

John: That would be fine, Dad. I haven't beaten you for several months now.

Dad: You won't beat me this time either. That crazy radio will destroy your balance as well as your hearing.

They both laugh and Dad thanks John for the time as he leaves. John smiles to himself as he turns the radio back up and goes back to his school book. Dad's trip to John's safe pad has been highly successful. The door of communication has been opened even wider. Do you know the safe pad of your adolescent? If not, try to find it. A trip there will prove to be an exciting adventure in relationship building.

Learn to Speak the Language

Some of the most difficult and frustrating times of my life have been times spent in countries where English is not spoken. I want to communicate, but it seems that the harder I try the less successful I am. Without my translator and a few English-speaking friends I would be totally confused.

Parents often express the same frustrations, saying, "I don't speak the same language as my teenager. It's so frustrating I could scream." Interestingly enough, the one time that parents and teens do speak the same language is when they are angry. Cutting words seem to move across communication barriers quite easily.

When I say, "Learn to speak the language," I do not mean that you should emulate your teenager's language or conduct. Parents are not expected to talk "adolescentese." They are expected to talk like adults. Trying to understand the talk and mannerisms of the adolescent enough to be able to communicate with them is helpful. Young people are not nearly as frightening as they seem, particularly when you hear what they are saying. Speak straight English to them. They will understand you. You will be delighted to learn that they will even help you understand their friends and others of this seemingly foreign culture.

Communication specialists have provided us with some very helpful tools in increasing communication effectiveness. One tool I have found to be helpful is called "learning channels." People do not all learn in the same way. Some people are visually oriented and learn by carefully visualizing things as they think. Other people are auditorily oriented. They may hear the thoughts or talk to themselves internally as they learn. Other learners are kinesthetic. They feel things or learn best through hands-on experience. Welter describes these learning channels well.

> One way to understand the concept of learning channels is to imagine that you live in a TV viewing area where you are able to get three channels, only one of which gives you good reception. A second channel is fair, although the fidelity may be poor and it may have some "snow." Let's suppose that the third channel is very weak. You have to work hard just to get the main idea of a given program on that channel. This is somewhat like learning channels, because often one may be strong and another weak.[2]

As you become aware of the way your adolescent learns, you will be able to communicate with him more effectively. If I approach my teenager, who is visually oriented, with just words, he doesn't understand me. If, however, I sketch out what I am trying to say, he gets my message right away. In this case one picture is worth a thousand words.

One of the easiest ways to determine which learning channel is strongest in yourself or your adolescent is to listen to the verbs and adverbs that are used. An auditory person will make reference to sounds or hearing, or will use adverbs like noisily, loudly, quietly, softly. A kinesthetic youngster may talk more about how things feel or about texture. Rather than trying to guess which channel is strongest or weakest, why not sit down as a family and talk about it? This exercise alone will be enough to get the communication process started. Make it a fun time, a time in which you all learn something about yourselves and each other.

Understand Your Adolescent's Personality Strengths

Communication with your teenager improves if you seek to understand his personality better. I have found it helpful to conceptualize personality in four interrelated aspects. This model is presented in Figure 6.

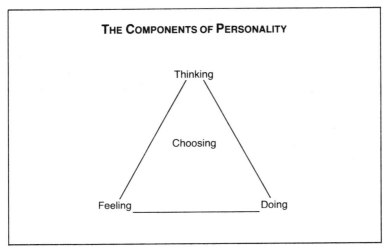

Figure 6

Choosing is placed in the center of the triangle because we make choices in each of the other three areas. We choose what to do, but we also choose what to think and what to feel. Often parents and teenagers are unaware of the importance of choice in the latter two areas. Melissa, age eleven, is upset by the actions of her younger sister and shouts, "You make me mad!" This is not a true statement. Michelle does things which Melissa does not like, but Michelle does not make Melissa angry. Melissa is choosing to be angry. We only kid ourselves if we think that thinking and feeling happen to us without any choice on our part.[3]

Determine Your Teen's Personality Strengths

Just as people differ in the strengths and weaknesses of their learning channels, they also differ in the strengths of their personality. Some people are strong thinkers. They figure things out logically and seem to enjoy playing with ideas. When they face a problem they often need space and time to think.

In the same family there may be a strong doer. This person is constantly active, making things, going places, working with puzzles. When a doer faces a problem, the worst possible curse would be to stay quiet and think things through.

A person who is a strong feeler is extra sensitive in the emotional area. My feeling child comes to me, for example, and says, "Dad, are you aware of how you made my brother feel?" "What do you mean?" I reply. "I just told him that he wasn't thinking clearly." A very common error that parents make is to deal with a doing child by logic or thoughts alone. Invariably this course of action leads to harsh, angry words. If you want to communicate, try walking and talking rather than sitting still. Don't tell him or her to do—do with him. Words make more sense when there is a meaningful activity going on at the same time.

I have observed that many adolescents are weak in the choice area and thus are not as effective as they might be in the other three areas. Decision making needs to be taught to teenagers just as they have need to be taught to drive the family car. If your teenagers are good decision makers, they will be self-confident and trustworthy. Help them learn how to make choices in all three areas.

One of the easiest ways to teach choice is to make them aware of the decisions you are making from day to day. As my daughter and I drive to town together, I sometimes tell her how I am struggling with a situation at work. I'll say, "I'm really trying not to be angry, but my other options aren't very clear sometimes." In this process I ask her what she would suggest. Sometimes she will come up with an amazingly good alternative. Thus, she helps me in the process of her own learning.

One caution must be given. Do not put the burden of your work or family matters on your children in such a way that they feel they must solve it. That is your job as a parent and the teenager needs that assurance. On the other hand, don't hide problems from them. They need to know that solutions are obtainable.

Approach Your Teen Via His Personality Strength

Whichever component in your child's personality is the strongest is the easiest wavelength to approach him on. He is not afraid to let you in if you knock at the strong door. If your child is strong in feeling, do not be afraid to allow him to express those feelings. To ignore his feelings is devastating to the relationship. Listen to understand and then you may be able to lead your child to some choice which will restore his sense of well-being. Remember, the way your child feels is the way it is for him or her at that moment. Asking him how he would like to feel rather than telling him how he should feel is much more effective.

One of my favorite illustrations of good communication that results from allowing the child to use his strengths is recorded in *Between Parent and Teenager.*

Here is a mother who used her skill to start the day on the right foot.

"The alarm went off, but Cyrus, age fifteen, shut it off, turned over and went back to sleep.

I called, 'Clock says seven-thirty, Cy.'

'I know,' he grumbled.

'It's rough getting out of bed, especially on a cool morning. How about a warm cup of cocoa?'

'NO, I'd rather have coffee and some toast—nothing else please.'

He was up. I didn't have to nag him or threaten him. But he was still grumpy. He complained,

'All these books. I get tired before the day begins.'

'You want a ride to school this morning, don't you?' I questioned.

'Well, yes,' he said, 'but I don't want to get you out of the house so early. I can't wait till I get my driver's license. I'll get myself a jalopy or a jeep and drive myself.' He got dressed and walked to school."[4]

Notice the strengthening of the relationship and the building of the teenager's self-understanding and self-esteem that results from this single interchange lasting less than thirty seconds.

Spiritual and Psychological Dualism

A word needs to be said about spiritual and psychological dualism.[5] In brief, this is a condition in which a person's feeling and thinking result in two separate patterns of doing, instead of feeling and thinking coming together in the choice of the unified behavior. Unified behavior and dualism are contrasted in Figure 7.

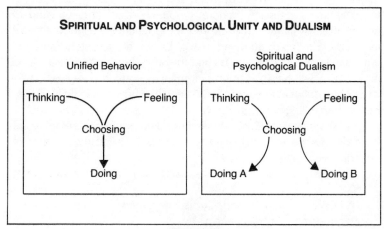

Figure 7

This dualistic pattern is seen in the life of Roger, a sixteen-year-old high school senior. Roger has strong religious values and strong moral standards which are a result of his thinking. He has been well indoctrinated in Christian ethics. Unfortunately, in this indoctrination process which emphasized thinking, Roger did not have an opportunity to discuss his feelings with either his parents or his youth group leaders. Therefore, Roger has one set of behaviors (Doing A) that says, "Be honest at all times. God will be with you." As a result of feelings, a second set of behaviors says, "Don't let people know who you really are or you will just get hurt" (Doing B). Roger vascillates back and forth and at times is very confused.

This dualism is beginning to destroy Roger's relationships with his parents, teachers, and peers. In the process Roger is developing a sense of guilt and self-hatred that are leading to severe depression. This dualism is avoidable if teenagers are encouraged to talk about all aspects of their person—thinking, feeling, choosing, and doing. The most helpful role of the parent is active listening and, when needed, challenging the adolescent's misconceptions without telling him what to do. When Roger's dad began to listen to him and to share some of his own struggles with honesty, Roger began to take some responsibility in this area.

Building Communication Bridges

Understanding your teenager's personality will enable you to be more empathetic as he deals with each struggle in life. You will probably find that as you struggle to know and understand, he will make more of an effort to really get to know you.

There is an anecdote which is told over and over in our culture about the person who at the age of fourteen couldn't believe how stupid his parents were, and who at age twenty-one couldn't believe how intelligent they had become. Maturity and emancipation allow a young person to see his parents as they really are. I believe this takes place any time an adolescent and a parent begin to understand each other to the point of listening and sharing, instead of playing silly power games.

If you want to communicate with your teenager, you must listen more than you talk. Seem to understand. Don't give advice. Learn to enter your adolescent's safe pad. Learn to speak your teenager's language, and get to know him as a person. You cannot do all of these things at once. You *can* do something. And whatever you do will help to build a bridge of communication.

Developing communication with teenagers is like writing a book. It isn't written in chapters. Books are written in words, phrases, sentences, paragraphs, pages, and then chapters. Communication is accomplished by listening and sharing, and listening and asking. Moment by moment and day by day bridges between you and your teenager can be built. *"Let us not become weary in doing good,"* Paul urges us, *"for at the proper time we will reap a harvest if we do not give up. Therefore, as we have opportunity, let us do good to all people, especially to those who belong to the family of God."* One parent persisted in *"doing good"* by trying to communicate with her son. She prayed: "I'm talking with him, Lord, and you know? I think I'm getting through!"

Footnotes

[1]Webster's New Collegiate Dictionary, 1979 ed., s.v. "communicate."
[2]Paul Welter, *Family Problems and Predicaments: How to Respond* (Wheaton, Ill.: Tyndale House Publishers, Inc., 1977), p. 212.
[3]This process is discussed in detail in chapter 6 of my book, *Faith and Personality,* to be published by InterVarsity Press.
[4]Haim G. Ginott, *Between Parent and Teenager* (New York: Avon Books, 1969), pp. 57-58.
[5]See *Faith and Personality,* chapter 3.

Chapter 7

Influencing Your Teenager's Spiritual Development

What do I do, God?
He just isn't spiritual.

If I had written the Bible I would have gone into much more detail. I would have told exactly how to raise a child, and I would have gone into the specifics about how to *"bring them up in the training and instruction of the Lord"* (Ephesians 6:4b). Please don't turn me off for irreverence. Even though I would like more detail in certain aspects of Scripture, I believe God knew exactly what He was doing.

A missionary friend pointed out to me that if the Bible gave specifics on training children, it would not be a universal book. Child rearing is cultural. The Bible supersedes culture. Our job is to take the universal guidelines God has given and then, through prayerful consultation with God, discover how to use those guidelines in raising our children.

This chapter will deal with discoveries that I, and others, have made which seem relevant to the task of helping our teenagers develop spirituality. There are no experts in this field. There are only fellow pilgrims to point you to paths that seem to be in the right direction.

The Basic Premise

The ideas presented here are based on the premise that God intended for the Christian message to be communicated via relationships. I believe in friendship evangelism, and in friendship as the greatest means of discipling others.[1] Jesus stated that, *"All men will know that you are my disciples if you love one another"* (John 13:35), and I believe family members are a part of *"all"* men. Loving relationships within the family are the greatest proof of the validity of the Gospel for your teenagers. They will believe and follow what they see practiced in the home. If adolescents see only hypocrisy within the home, they will develop disdain for the "faith" of their parents.

This is not to say that parents have to be perfect in order to positively influence the spiritual development of their adolescents. Teenagers are brighter than that. They both know and understand failure. What they don't understand is *not trying* to live by faith. They don't understand an attitude that says something is important and yet never does anything about it. Yancey and Stafford write about this in *Unhappy Secrets of the Christian Life.*

> A hypocrite is someone who says he believes one thing but lives another. By that standard I am a hypocrite, and so are you. In fact, there is no one who claims to be a Christian who is not in one sense a hypocrite. Did not Jesus tell us, "You shall love the Lord your God with all your mind, soul and strength, and your neighbor as yourself?" And don't we agree that those words are the standard for life? But none of us lives up to those words. The greatest difference between me and Mr. Thomas is not whether or not I live up to my beliefs; on that score I am a failure too. The difference is in the attitude toward that failure.[2]

The greatest vehicle for influencing your teenager's spiritual development is the relationship that you have with them. This relationship will be effective as you convey an attitude of wanting to honor God. Unfortunately, many parents who are believers fail to create a relationship where the parents, the teenagers, and God are all part of a mutual friendship system. Both teenagers and parents need to relate to God separately, but they also need to relate to God corporately. This type of relationship is pictured in Figure 8.

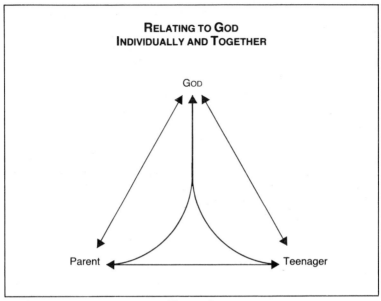

RELATING TO GOD
INDIVIDUALLY AND TOGETHER

GOD

Parent   Teenager

Figure 8

Each relationship specified by the arrows has the potential of strengthening the other relationships. For example, if the parent is relating to God individually, this provides a better basis for relating to the teenager individually, and for the two of them to relate to God together. Furthermore, relating to God together may be a source of encouragement for you to relate to God individually. Teenagers sometimes find praying in private easier when they have learned to pray, and expect God to answer, by praying with a parent.

Steps for Promoting Spiritual Growth in Your Teen

Parents often ask me to tell them something that they can do to help their teenager.

1. Be an Example
At the risk of over-simplifying matters, let me suggest six things that you as a parent can do to encourage your teenager to grow spiritually. Remember that each of these steps are based on a growing parent-teen relationship. The first step for growth that I explain to parents is always the hardest: *Be an example!* More Christian living is learned by

watching parents than from attending school, or hearing sermons. Adolescents read you like a book.

Personally, I am often frustrated because I find it so easy to demonstrate a lack of faith and self-control. On the other hand, I know by watching all my children just how important my example is.

Your adolescents watch you in every area: what you say, what you do, and how you demonstrate love, faith, and morality. Rather than being frightened by this, see it as an opportunity. Too often we only look at the negative side. Your adolescent wants to be proud of your spirituality. Even if your life is not perfect, the example is still effective.

Sandy and I had an opportunity to work for a summer in upper British Columbia. We met a delightful family who had become Christians after the children were all over age ten. Previously their lives had been very rough. They had been examples of various things, but none of them spiritual. Their daughter volunteered to help us teach Bible school classes, so we took her with us each day about thirty miles to a small town where we were teaching.

As we drove, we asked her questions about her family. When asked about her brother she said, "Jake doesn't live at home. He left because he and my dad had a fight once." I said, "Does that worry you?" She just smiled and said, "No! It's okay! My dad is praying for him now and he will be back. You see, when my dad prays, things happen." I was challenged to see how good an example this rugged new believer was to the people that needed his example the most, his children.

2. Be Public About Your Faith

A related growth step is *being public about your faith.* Don't shelter your teenagers from the realities of day-to-day Christian living. When we lived in Iran, we had an opportunity to adopt Melissa, who was born in the "backyard" of the biblical characters Esther and Mordecai. The only problem was that Iranian law had no provisions for such an adoption. We prayed with our children and were open about the difficulties we faced. We didn't realize the impact of those prayers until, after several small miracles, we received the necessary papers permitting us to bring her home with us. I will never forget Marcy, our oldest daughter, swinging Melissa around and around the room that day. She said, "Isn't it wonderful what God has done? Now no one can ever take you away from us." Being public about the struggle had helped Marcy get a clear picture of the faithfulness of God.

Even though I know how faithful God is, I sometimes want to protect Him a little just in case He slips up and doesn't answer a prayer.

Obviously my lack of faith is showing. God will protect His reputation. Our only job is to love and enjoy His great faithfulness. God taught me this through another incident with Marcy.

When Marcy was about ten, we owned a pair of Samoyeds and were raising puppies. Marcy prayed that all the puppies would live. I was uneasy about such a specific prayer, as I am often uncertain about how God works in such matters. When the puppies were born there were nine of them, eight very healthy ones and one that appeared to me to be dead or dying.

After some soul searching, I decided to dispose of the puppy before Marcy got home from school. I put him in the wastebasket and started out. I stopped about halfway up the stairs and realized I couldn't do it. Deception just isn't a good way to promote spiritual development. I took the puppy back to the mother and went to get her some food. When I came back the mother had the puppy in her mouth. My first thought was, "Oh no, she's eating him!" I then realized that she was trying to revive him.

When I came back with fresh water a little later I counted the puppies and there were nine. I was shaking. I sat down to pray. I confessed my lack of faith and praised God that He was so faithful. When Marcy got home from school she said, "I knew God would take care of our puppies! Aren't they cute?"

As we are public with our teenagers about our faith, they see that God really works in our lives. If we pray only in private, they will not have an opportunity to see how God works. As you are public with them, you will also have an opportunity to deal with the apparent lack of answers to prayer, and the doubts and fears that arise. This, too, is a part of influencing spiritual development, as John Lavender writes.

> It is easy to have faith—when you are sick and ask for healing, and it comes. It is not difficult to believe in prayer—when you are caught up in trouble and plead for guidance, and you receive it. Anyone can trust in God—when, having petitioned heaven for the protection of a loved one, he sees that one come through unscathed. But when you ask for healing and it does not come . . . when you pray for guidance and you do not get it . . . when you plead some causes and the heavens seem as brass—then it is not so easy to have faith.[3]

In reality no sincere prayer is ever unanswered. The problem is that sometimes the answer is no.

We often struggle with God when He tells us no or when He is slow to act—just as our teenagers struggle with us when we don't grant their every request.

Young people are too smart to believe that anything as important as one's relationship with God happens automatically without any questions or struggles. What they need is the opportunity to see how these struggles have affected their parents. Through this involvement growth takes place.

3. Develop Dialogue

The opportunity to observe the parent's faith leads to the third growth promoting step, *dialogue between the parent and the teen.* Dialogue is best defined as "talking with." It is not "talking to" or "talking at." Dialogue is an interchange between persons who, at that moment, share equal status. If I am to dialogue with my teenagers, I must believe that their perceptions of the situation are valid. Otherwise the interchange will turn into a lecture and little, if any, growth will take place.

Ask your teenagers what they think about unanswered prayer, for example. Don't tell them what they should think. As you share honestly, their insights will be helpful to you, and your ideas will be helpful to them. When both opinions are accepted, then turn to the Bible together and be taught by the Holy Spirit. When the views of the adolescent are not accepted, attempts to bring in the Scripture are seen only as an imposition of the parent's point of view. The answer to the problem comes when we replace monologue (telling our teenagers) with dialogue (talking with our teenager).

The importance of listening, understanding, and caring for the other person needs to be understood if dialogue is to take place. Dialogue is an adult-to-adult proposition. As a parent, if you fall back into the parent-to-child interaction, you will lose the very thing you seek—the opportunity to promote spiritual growth. Dialogue is best fulfilled by asking questions, not by giving answers. You don't need to have things all put together in order to have a positive impact on your teenager's spiritual development. Your role is to be a consultant, not a repair person. Consultants help point out the problem. They don't take on the responsibility of fixing everything.

When Jesus interacted with the disciples, He often asked many questions and was able to build on the answers which He received. For example, in Matthew 16:13-16, we do not find Jesus giving the disciples a lecture on His identity as the Son of God. Instead, we discover Jesus asking questions to prod their thinking about His true identity. It was only then that Peter declared, " *'You are the Christ, the Son of the living God' "* (Matthew 16:16). In the same way, a parent can expand a teenager's thinking by asking questions in the normal course of events, instead of forcing the teenagers to put up with a lecture now and then.

One of the functions of a good counseling relationship is to help the client unravel or expand emotions which have become tangled or compacted. Good dialogue between parent and adolescent fulfills this same important function. Spiritual growth is often inhibited by the fact that the adolescent has difficulty relating facts and feelings. The teenager may show amazing understanding intellectually, but be very confused about spiritual matters emotionally. Patient dialogue provides the atmosphere in which this confusion can be unraveled.

One of the ways a parent helps unravel feelings is to listen for reoccurring themes. Often things that are implied in several ways over a period of time give more insight into the adolescent's spiritual needs than the direct statements which are made. These themes will surface if you as parent and friend dialogue with your teenager rather than monologue *at* him or her. Sue put it very well. "It sure is more helpful when my parents talk with me rather than just telling me what to believe."

4. Deal with Issues Squarely

Another important factor in promoting spriritual development is *dealing with issues squarely.* Christianity presents very few intellectual problems which cannot be handled by the average parent who is willing to search the Bible and other books for an answer. Parents sometimes avoid this responsibility because they themselves have doubts, and they do not want to rock anyone's boat. John Stott writes about the importance of seeking God's thoughts on the issues of the day.

> That God needs to take the initiative to reveal Himself shows that our minds are finite and fallen; that He chooses to reveal Himself to babies shows that we must humble ourselves to receive His Word; that He does so at all, and in words, shows that our minds are capable of understanding it. One of the highest and noblest functions of man's mind is to listen to God's Word, and so to read His mind and think His thoughts after Him, both in nature and in Scripture.[4]

Parents need to let their young people search for answers, rather than to spoon-feed them. If the adolescent is encouraged and supported in dealing with critical issues while in the safe environment of the Christian home, the challenges presented by unbelieving college professors will have much less impact. On the other hand, adolescents sheltered from some of the difficult intellectual questions will be vulnerable to the attacks presented by agnostic or atheistic teachers.

One young man said, "My parents really ripped me off! They never told me about some of the problems I would have to face." In contrast, the Scriptures urge us to grapple for answers to the issues of the day: *"But in your hearts set apart Christ as Lord. Always be prepared to give an answer to everyone who asks you to give the reason for the hope that you have"* (1 Peter 3:15).

If you, as a parent, are willing to discuss difficult issues with your teenagers, you will prepare them to give an answer, even if you don't have all the answers yourself. Fellow strugglers can learn much from each other.

Another area where issues need to be squarely dealt with is in the moral or ethical arena. I called my wife last week to tell her I was on my way home from work. Casually I said, "How did your afternoon go?" "Fine," she said, "if you like teaching two teenagers about sex and values. I didn't get anything else done after they got home from school, but I think it was worth it." Marcy and John, both age seventeen, had been in a mood to unload their questions, and their mom was up to the task. She was exhausted, but warmly satisfied by the interaction. Her teaching had been effective because she listened to their point of view without being put off by the fact that they asked about things which make parents uncomfortable.

Although it is difficult for parents to see their teenagers struggle with whether to do right or wrong, the fact that they let you in on the struggle is most encouraging. If you are not condemning them, you can teach them important truths about God's love and forgiveness as well as His standards.

When I was a youth leader of our church I went to visit a young man who had been placed in the Juvenile Detention Home because he had stolen money at school. I went in and sat with him, and I could tell that he was very uncomfortable. "Ron," I said, "can God forgive you for what you did?" "I think so," he replied. When we finished praying, his face was relaxed and he was open to new input and interaction. He was encouraged because I believed that he wanted to do the right thing, even though he had sinned by stealing.

When I first read Romans 7:18b-24, I thought Paul must have been a teenager when he wrote it. Now that I am older, I see he must have written it as an adult.

For I have the desire to do what is good, but I cannot carry it out. For what I do is not the good I want to do; no, the evil I do not want to do—this I keep on doing. Now if I do what I do not want to do, it is no longer I who do it, but it is sin living in me that does it. So I find this law at work: When I want to do good, evil is right there with me. For in my inner being I delight in God's law; but I see another law at work in the members of my body, waging war against the law of my mind and making me a prisoner of the law of sin at work within my members. What a wretched man I am! Who will rescue me from this body of death?

Be honest enough with your young people to let them know that you also struggle. You will find a tremendous source of support as you deal with difficult issues together. Their emotions will ebb and flow as yours do, but the result will be greater stability because issues have been squarely faced.

5. Integrate Christianity into Life

A fifth factor to encourage spiritual development is to *help the young people integrate their church activities into their total life situation.* I am not calling for control or domination. I am suggesting wise guidance. Most young people are overloaded with homework, school activities, sports, music lessons, and several church activities each week. Even though their energy supply seems unlimited, their inability to say "No" causes them to do too much and to enjoy too little.

Rather than wait for a crisis and then lecture them on the perils of doing too much, it is helpful to look ahead and help your teens to evaluate the situation. A question like, "Do you feel you are going to be able to enjoy yourself if you are overloaded?" frees the adolescent to think about cutting back. This fosters questions like, "Dad, what do you think I should cut out?" But don't answer the question, even if you have a good idea. Force them to evaluate. "What's important to you, Son?" is a good question to ask.

If youth activities get left out, help them to see that by saying something like, "You seem to like your youth group. Will you need to eliminate it? Maybe you could drop one school function and one thing at church so that you could survive the month." You are not teaching them to drop church. You are only teaching them to set priorities, which is a function of spiritual growth.

John Alexander, President of Inter-Varsity Christian Fellowship, has pointed out that, "You cannot be a mature Christian until you learn to say 'No.' " Helping your teenager to set priorities will enable him to have the time to grow in his faith. Otherwise he might grow up to be like the average Christian church person—over-involved, under-joyed, and perhaps even bitter.

Parents also must carefully regulate their involvements so that they have time for their teenagers. A young man who was raised in a staunch Christian home said, "God is a thief! I don't think He loves me at all! He took my parents from me. They were never home when I needed them. They were always at church." When in doubt, ask your children if you are too involved. Let them serve as *your* teenager consultant and advisor in this area, just as you desire to do so for them.

6. Help Them Develop Other Adult Friends

A sixth area of importance in prioritizing spiritual growth is *putting your young person in touch with spiritually-oriented, caring adults.* Psychologist Garry Powell, formerly of Young Life, has stated, "I feel it is almost impossible for a Christian teenager to make it today without the support of an adult friend." Young people need to link themselves to strong Christian values, but this link is not always provided by their parents. There are too many hooks in parent-teen relationships which prevent the young person from taking advantage of the adult perspective.

We are extremely grateful for the friendships provided for our children by caring Christian adults, who spend time with them and encourage them to be all they can be in their relationship with Christ. Parents often blow it because they are too critical. Adult friends are often capable of being more supportive and yet just as effective in their guidance. Sometimes I feel churches should sponsor trade-a-teen day. Both parents and young people would benefit and also be more appreciative of their own home situation.

Our son, Mark, was invited to spend a week with his adult friend, Pete, who was a youth pastor in West Yellowstone. Mark came back from the time challenged and refreshed. Pete had a significant impact on his life and the two of them had a great time. As a family we have tried to reciprocate by reaching out to teens in addition to our own. The scriptural admonition to *"encourage one another"* (Hebrews 10:25) needs to cross the generation barrier. As an adult, you will probably need to take the first steps, whether in assisting or enabling your teen to find adult friends, or in reaching out to other teenagers yourself.

Hindrances to Teenage Spirituality

In the Christian community we have a tendency to define spirituality in terms of minutes prayed, or chapters read from the Bible, or verses memorized. In our desire to pass our spiritual life on to our teenagers, we often set standards for them which we ourselves do not keep. When they are not successful in meeting our criteria, they become discouraged and feel guilty for "letting God down." We respond with more pressure and they respond with more guilt. The situation becomes hopeless . . . and getting worse.

Unrealistic Expectations

As I think of my own experience as a teenager, I realize that my adult friends helped deliver me from the pit of feeling like a failure because I sometimes neglected God. My teachers helped me to focus on what I was doing and learning, and not on the negative. I was encouraged to live my life with an awareness that God was there. This in my judgment is spirituality. Rather than *how much* you know, it's *who* you know. It's not how much you pray, but that you pray. If we are to promote spiritual life with our teens, we need to be positive. God understands the process of growth much better than we do. He is also more patient.

I believe the model of spiritual growth presented in 2 Peter 1:5-9 is the model we should present to our teens. After carefully listing some of the goals toward which we should strive—faith, goodness, knowledge, self-control, perseverance, godliness, brotherly kindness, and love—Peter writes: *"For if you possess these qualities in increasing measure, they will keep you from being ineffective and unproductive in your knowledge of our Lord Jesus Christ"* (2 Peter 1:8).

The key phrase is "in increasing measure." Have an attitude of wanting to grow. Most teenage believers I have met have such an attitude, at least early in their Christian experience. They can and will grow if they are encouraged to take baby steps and to enjoy them as they learn to walk. We often encourage teenage Christians to be adults before they are able to walk as children.

Dr. Earl Radmacher, President of Western Conservative Baptist Seminary, tells of listening to a group of youth pastors talk about a recently completed Bible camp. One pastor said that a young man had committed himself to reading the Bible for two hours every day. All the other pastors replied by saying how great that was. Dr. Radmacher said, "I couldn't help myself! I jumped to my feet and said, 'How awful! No teenager will keep that kind of commitment! He will only end up feeling like a failure!' "

I agree with this point of view. We need to encourage teens to read and pray, but we cannot impose an impossible standard on them. The Holy Spirit will be active in their lives, giving them an appetite for the things of God. As parents, we need to pray and read with our teenagers and encourage them to pray and read for themselves. The amount is not nearly as important as remaining centered on the fact that God wants us to live moment by moment with Him in mind. In his book *True Spirituality,* Francis Schaeffer writes about the danger of unrealistic expectations or standards.

The alternatives are not between being perfect or being nothing. Just as people smash marriages because they are looking for what is romantically and sexually perfect and in this poor world do not find it, so human beings often smash what could have been possible in a true church or true Christian group. It is not just the "they" involved who are not yet perfect, but the "I" is not yet perfect either. In the absence of present perfection, Christians are to help each other on to increasingly substantial healing on the basis of the finished work of Christ.[5]

Parental Unwillingness

If you desire to promote spiritual development in the life of your teenager, you need to share your spiritual life with him or her. Be open and available. You must also be prepared to accept the challenge that results from their being more spiritual than you. We are warned in Scripture not to be a spiritual stumbling block: *"But if anyone causes one of these little ones who believe in me to sin, it would be better for him to have a large millstone hung around his neck and to be drowned in the depths of the sea. Woe to the world because of the things that cause people to sin! Such things must come, but woe to the man through whom they come!"* (Matthew 18:6-7). Parents cause their teenagers to stumble by holding them back when they want to go forward in their Christian life. Ask yourself if you are willing to have your teenager totally dedicated to Christ. The answer you find may shock you.

Footnotes

¹See *Life-Style Evangelism* by Joseph C. Aldrich (Portland: Multnomah Press, 1981).

²Philip Yancey and Tim Stafford, *Unhappy Secrets of the Christian Life* (Wheaton, Ill.: Campus Life Books, 1979), p. 152.

³John Allan Lavender, *Why Prayers Are Unanswered* (Valley Forge: Judson Press, 1967), p. 15.

⁴John R. W. Stott, *Your Mind Matters* (Downers Grove, Ill.: InterVarsity Press, 1972), pp. 20-21.

⁵Francis A. Schaeffer, *True Spirituality* (Wheaton, Ill.: Tyndale House Publishers, 1972), pp. 179-80.

Chapter 8

Dealing with Conflicts in Values and Moral Standards

They know better, God.
How could they?

As an evangelical Christian, I have been shocked to realize that on tests of moral development that are used extensively, Christians do not score differently than non-Christians. In fact, in many instances the level of moral functioning for Christians seems to be lower than the level exhibited by many who do not profess a Christian faith. Without becoming defensive about the test, which has some flaws, I have sought to understand why we as Christian parents are not having a bigger impact on the moral development of our children. Although the answers are quite complex, I believe they provide us with some helpful guidelines for interacting with our teenagers.

When I remove my professional hat and consider the problem "as just a parent," I am no less concerned. "They know better, God. How could they?" we ask ourselves. "What did I do wrong? What am I doing wrong? How can I do things differently?" For most parents, retreating to the safe notion that society is changing is not enough. If our values are not good, then why do we cling to them? We want our children to experience and live that which we feel is right. Why then do we seem to be pulling in different directions?

In recent years, the process called values clarification has come under widespread attack because of the humanistic implications. Without debating the relative merits of this process, let me say that parents and teenagers need help in understanding what their values are. My experience has shown that for many people, values are academic rather than practical guides for living. We often report that we believe one thing and yet resort to living quite differently. It is important to examine your own value structure, and to be able to help your teenager determine what he believes and why.

How Values and Moral Standards Are Acquired

Close your eyes for a moment and remember the days when your child would flood you with hundreds of "Why?" questions. "Why do birds fly? Why do I have to eat my peas? Why doesn't Jesus go to church? Why do I have to go to Sunday School? Why do I have to share my candy?" Although you may not have realized it, in trying to respond to these and countless other questions, you were performing an important function in helping your child acquire values. "Why?" questions are basic to values formation and should be answered whenever possible. These answers form the rationale for the child's development of a system of values as Feather observes.

When considering the development of adolescent values, it is important to take account of both children's emerging capacities and their active role as processors of information. Children are not passive receivers, molded like clay by outside forces, but are actively involved in interpreting, constructing, and transforming experience in a unique way, influenced by the nature of the information that they encounter and by their level of maturity.[1]

The child no sooner gets used to asking "Why?" then he changes and becomes the authority. "You shouldn't do that! It isn't fair! He is bad! That isn't right!" Along with these two periods of active learning, the youngster is constantly receiving input both formally and informally from other sources: parents, teachers, church, and friends. The young person is constantly receiving input regarding right and wrong and good and evil. The mind of the young person is flooded with information. Unfortunately, much of the information seems contradictory and confusing.

As though this situation were not bad enough, youngsters also get more information by observing those persons who are close to them. Children tend to value what they see their parents valuing. If there happens to be consistency between what the parents *say* they value and what they *show*, this value will become strong in the life of the child. If there is no consistency, the child will become even more confused. Sometime during the life of a young person he has to stop and sort this all out. They often turn to their peers as authorities, only to find other teens as confused as they are.

I believe that much of the emotional upheaval that young people exhibit traces back to confusion over values and moral standards. Some try to resolve the confusion by rebelling and not believing in anything. Others try to submit to their parents' value structure, even though they see some inconsistencies. James Marcia has referred to this as a crisis period in the development of the adolescent. He writes: "Crisis refers to times during adolescence when the individual seems to be actively involved in choosing among alternative occupations and beliefs."[2]

Adolescence is the great period of questioning. It is the period of deciding for one's self. I call adolescence the parent's second chance. The adolescent is now able to reason and, with patient parental support, will decide on values for himself. Some values will be cast off but other values will be acquired. The great Jesus movement of the 1970s showed us that adolescence is not just a time of throwing off old values, but also a time when more traditional values are sometimes sought and accepted. Parents have a second chance because adolescents often look beyond their parents' mistakes, and acquire values for themselves which their parents displayed in a very imperfect manner.

It is also a second chance if the parents realize that the rules have changed. Adolescents are no longer open to being *told,* but they are still open to being *shown.* In fact, they long to see positive demonstrations of the values and beliefs which they have been inclined to hold. (This point will be discussed again later.)

This description of how values are acquired is obviously sketchy and incomplete. My purpose is to show the various changes that you as a parent can anticipate. I have purposely omitted ages since your child may not fit the pattern. Observe what is happening right now and discuss this with your child. They will be amused by the fact that you recognize that they no longer like to be told what to do. Ask them how they would like you to interact with them about some of these issues. You will learn a great deal and some doors of opportunity for a closer relationship will open. This is the only sure way to grasp the changing nature of the process of values acquisition which your adolescent is going through.

Factors in Imparting Values

Let's summarize the various stages of the process of acquiring values. The process from direct parental action to internalized values is described by Berkowitz below.

> When he is very young, of course, the child must be controlled by direct parental action. The mother must prevent her child from touching the hot stove. . . . As he gets older, he learns that his parents want him to do certain things at certain times and not to do other things. He gets approval for carrying out the desired actions and some form of punishment if he departs from his parents' standards. . . . This type of self-control is, however, ultimately based on the anticipation of detection; the child carries out the desired action or avoids the prohibited behavior because he believes that the people who can reward or punish him will find out what he has done. It is not until he has truly internalized parental and societal moral standards that he will behave in a socially proper fashion solely because this is the "right" thing to do.[3]

When you read this statement, it becomes obvious that if you, as a parent, want to impart values, you must be aware of the stage which your child is in and react to your child in such a way as to teach him the next step. In this section I will present some positive actions for you to take in accomplishing this task.

1. Be Explicit about Your Own Values

I cannot overstate the importance of knowing what you believe before you even consider what you want to impart to your children. You cannot avoid teaching values. The question is, which values do you want to teach? If your values are functional for you, then why not be explicit about them to yourself as well as your children?

One of our Christian friends discovered a copy of *Playboy* magazine under her son's mattress. The mother was shocked. The father reacted calmly but did not avoid his responsibility. He sat down with his son to talk. The conversation went something like this: "I understand you have been trying to catch up on your sex education by looking at *Playboy*." In a somewhat subdued manner the son said, "Yeah, but I just have one." The father's response was not condemning or designed to produce guilt. "I'd like to tell you why I decided not to read magazines like *Playboy*." He then went on to state his values in a positive manner. His son was free to listen because he had not been put on the defensive. The son also had the opportunity to see how his father had dealt with the ever present problem of sexual temptation.[4]

Adolescents do not experience much moral development through punishment, but they grow by leaps and bounds when parents are willing to share why they have made certain decisions. My friend's son was not only influenced by what his dad said, but was proud of his dad for the way he dealt with the matter.

Being explicit about your values does not mean that you will demand compliance on every point. There are, however, some issues which you may be rather demanding on. My father was uncompromising on such things as stealing—even a peanut at the store or an apple from the neighbor's tree. He also demanded absolute respect for my mother. I call him "blessed" because he had the strength to be explicit and even demanding in these and other very important areas. I also call him "blessed" because he let me work through many other areas on my own. He was there to share his point of view, but did not demand adherence to all his standards. He seemed to understand the changing world in which I was growing up.

2. State Clearly Where You Are

If I am explicit about my values, I must state them. This is particularly important since early in life young people become involved in the process of comparison and evaluation. "Tom talks back to his father. Why can't I?" "The Jones kids don't have to do chores." "Jimmy's dad didn't punish him for taking the watermelon. How come I got grounded?" Questions like these demand a clear, nonapologetic statement of the value structure from which you are operating. Teenagers don't mind being different if they understand the issues.

The identity formation of the young person is often facilitated by developing his awareness of the values and standards which you as an individual or family hold. Our friends, Dallas and Dorothy Keck, taught their children that worshiping God was a family value. I overheard one of their older children say, "We are the Kecks and we like to go to church." Each of their children still holds this value and the ones who are married are stating it and passing it along to their children.

Sandy and I have tried to respond to the "Why?" questions in a matter-of-fact, nondefensive way. "Why do we have to help with the housework?" we are asked sometimes, for instance.

"Because Wilsons like to share the load," we explain. "We want you to learn to be good workers."

"But other people don't have to work!"

"That's okay. They may not have a chance to learn some of the important things you are learning."

I believe that if you are reasonable in your demands, and positive in your attitudes, the positive statement of values will result in a sense of pride in the values and in being a part of the family.

Compare the family to school spirit for a minute. Children love to gripe about their school. They tell each other how dumb the school is and how bad the teachers are and yet they chant, "We're from Oregon City and couldn't be prouder. If you can't hear us now we'll yell a little louder." Clearly stating values, and establishing a family identity around these values, helps to develop a spirit of family comradeship.

3. Establish Discipline Patterns Related to Values

When I was about twelve years old, an early adolescent, I destroyed some property that belonged to other people. This hurt my father deeply since one of his strong values is respect for the rights and property of others. He did not become theatrical in dealing with the matter. He did not even try to make me feel guilty. He knew that I knew that what I had done was wrong. He did, however, discipline me for doing that which was contrary to our values—the values Dad and Mom were trying to teach. In the process he also taught me another value—the value of restoration. He paid for the damage that I had done. He didn't tell me how dearly it cost him. I knew. As I think over this incident, I admire his ability to keep the focus on the issue, rather than to try to create pity for himself. He was responsible, and instead of seeking pity, he wanted me to learn these values as well.

Good discipline is not based on punishment. Good discipline is based on helping the teenager learn the relationship between certain behavior and specific consequences. I learned that because I had destroyed property which had to be replaced, the family and I did not get to do certain things we otherwise could have done. There just wasn't enough money to go around. I was also restricted. I learned that freedom must be earned by demonstration of responsibility. I wasn't restricted forever. I was restricted long enough for the connection between freedom and responsibility to be fixed in my mind.

When discipline is applied to teach values, explaining "Why" is important: "I disapprove because. . . . This is wrong because. . . . This is good because. . . ." Don't just tell "Why," *ask* "Why?" so that the adolescent discovers the basis for his own values. My dad often asked me, "Do you know why I punished you?" or "Do you know why I want you to be home by midnight?" These questions, and others like them, were helpful to me as I began to internalize my own values. They were particularly helpful when they were associated with appropriate discipline when family values were violated.

Values and moral standards cannot be taught without consistent discipline. Consistency is much more important than severity. My parents rarely punished me severely, but they did discipline me consistently. I grew up knowing that certain behavior on my part resulted in certain consequences. This was and is most helpful.

4. Consistently Demonstrate Your Values

"Show me your faith without deeds, and I will show you my faith by what I do. . . . You foolish man, do you want evidence that faith without deeds is useless?" (James 2:18b, 20). Although these verses of Scripture relate to demonstrating faith, they could just as well have been written about the need to demonstrate values. You need to show your teenager your values by what you do. Indeed, values are rarely learned from what people say unless they are demonstrated. Stating values without demonstration is useless.

To my amazement I have discovered that many people spend hours trying to unravel the confusion that results from growing up with parents who *stated* one set of values and *lived* another. Living in such an environment results in confusion and sometimes even psychological maladjustment. I have labeled this problem "spiritual and psychological dualism." The person intellectually believes one set of values but emotionally responds quite differently.[5]

We often take values for granted without clearly demonstrating to our teenagers how one acts if one has certain values. There is no doubt in the minds of my children that I value church, sports, their mother's affection, and being honest with money. They go with me to church. They see me at sporting events. They watch me kiss their mother. They see me drive back to the store when I receive too much change. They know I do these things for me. I feel good about being what I value. Occasionally they will ask, "Why did you give back the money? You didn't have to." I usually respond by saying, "That's right! I didn't have to. I wanted to because God wants me to be honest and I feel good about myself when I am honest. You try it sometime and tell me how it makes you feel." These clear cut demonstrations are invaluable if you expect to impart your values to your children.

Don't be afraid to share your failures with your children. They need to see your honesty. They know you aren't perfect. As they see you struggle with hard decisions, they realize that they will also struggle, but that we all are able to make good decisions. God chose to show us the weaknesses and struggles of Moses, David, Paul, and Peter. He even showed us the temptation of Jesus. He would not have done this if it were not for our edification and personal growth. Help your adolescents grow by showing them the same type of honesty. Live your values in front of them. If you see that your values are not consistent or need shaping up, say so and let your teenager in on the process. They will love you for it, and you will find a deep sense of respect for them.

5. Direct Your Teenagers to Use Their Values in Making Decisions

If there is one characteristic that teenagers seem to demonstrate consistently, it is impulsiveness. They constantly leap before they look. You can see this in their driving. You see it in their friendship patterns, and you see it in their misuse of drugs and alcohol. How will they learn a better way if we don't teach them?

Psychological studies of self-control have taught us that the first step in self-control is determining how you want to behave. This obviously involves relating values to the decisions you make. Five steps for developing self-control in order to act responsibly are elaborated below.

Self-control procedures not only embody ethical and humanistic values, but they can also be very effective. Individuals take responsibility for changing some aspects of their own behavior. Their responsibility generally involves some or all of five basic components: selection of their own goals, monitoring their own behavior, selection of procedures for behavior change, implementation of the procedures, and evaluation of the effectiveness of the procedures.[6]

Teenagers, like adults, often make decisions on pragmatic grounds, rather than carefully considering how the specific decision fits into their overall pattern of goals, beliefs, or values. When faced with a decision we need to ask, "What kind of person do I want to be?" We sometimes tell our children, "Jesus wouldn't be pleased," but we seldom build the necessary bridges between God's standards, family values, personal values, and individual decisions. This concept is presented in Figure 9.

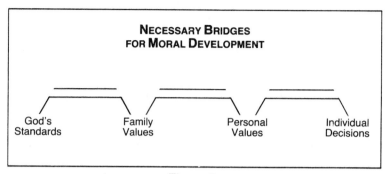

Figure 9

Good decision making requires that we ask questions which will direct us to consider the moral implications of each decision we make. This does not come naturally for either adults or teenagers. Making decisions is a skill which needs to be taught. Teach your teenagers to ask themselves, "What outcome would I like to see? What kind of person would I like to be in this situation? What action on my part would be consistent with my Christian life?" Each of the questions will result in a greater internalization of values and thus greater consistency of behavior related to morals and values. By helping your teenager to acquire these skills, you will help them to act correctly more often and to avoid the pitfall of having to learn everything the hard way.

Teenagers have values that are important to them. They just need to be helped to use their values before they decide, rather than feeling guilty afterward because they didn't think things through. Parents often add to the guilt factor when it is too late, rather than encouraging consideration of values while there is still time. If you are close to your teenager, you will have many opportunities for input *before* a problem arises, rather than after it's too late. My daughter said, "Thanks, Dad, I want to think about those things, but they don't always come to me." Openness and acceptance, without being critical, seem to be the key if parents desire the opportunity to interact with teenagers at this level.

6. Use Encouragement
The Bible is explicit about the need to use encouragement in our relationships within the family of God. This is made very clear in Hebrews 10:24-25. *"And let us consider how we may spur one another on toward love and good deeds. Let us not give up meeting together, as some are in the habit of doing, but let us encourage one another— and all the more as you see the Day approaching."*

If encouragement is important in the church, then it is just as important in the family.

My experience has shown that many people would like to be more encouraging, but they do not know how. What is encouragement and how can we do it? Dreikurs and Grey bring the issues into focus.

> Essentially, encouragement involves the ability to accept the child as worthwhile, regardless of any deficiency, and to assist him in developing his capacity and potentialities. . . . Specifically, the person who encourages: 1) places value on the child as he is; 2) shows faith in the child and enables him to have faith in himself; 3) sincerely believes in the child's ability and wins his confidence while building his self-respect; 4) recognizes a job "well done," gives recognition for effort; 5) utilizes the group to facilitate and enhance the development of the child; 6) integrates the group so that each student can be sure of his place in it; 7) assists in the development of the skills sequentially and psychologically based to permit success; 8) recognizes and focuses on strength and assets; and 9) utilizes the interest of the child to energize instruction.[7]

Each aspect of encouragement that is emphasized above requires that you, as a parent, get close to your teenager. You need to discover the wavelength that he is on. Encouragement requires that you be close and available without smothering. One of the greatest tools of encouragement is to provide positive feedback regarding the progress you see in the child. Let him know when his moral standards challenge you in the good way. Why assume that all good things start with parental authority? God always has and always will work in and through children. The Psalmist wrote: *"From the lips of children and infants you have ordained praise because of your enemies, to silence the foe and the avenger"* (Psalm 8:2).

Encouragement requires careful planning. Take your teenager out for a Coke and ask him what things you do that are encouraging. Then plan to do more of those things. So often we neglect encouragement because we mistakenly believe that we are encouraging when we reward success. The successes don't need encouragement. The effort that doesn't appear to have panned out needs to be encouraged. Young people need to be helped to understand that moral decisions or decisions that follow good values do not always have an immediate reward. Doing right for right's sake is very lonely if you do not feel that others are behind you. Parents must also recognize that doing right does not always feel good for the adolescent. This is especially true in light of peer pressures and the adolescent's lack of confidence in himself.

Encouragement requires that you focus on the positive, while acknowledging that it is difficult for the teenager. The standard is progress, not perfection. In 1980 professional baseball player George Brett was seeking to become the first person since Ted Williams to bat over .400 for an entire season. His quest for this achievement captivated the minds of many people who previously were only nominal baseball fans. Do you realize what Brett was trying to do? He was trying to make an out less than six out of ten times. His accomplishment was considered phenomenal even though he was only forty percent effective. Our abilities to encourage our teenagers will be greatly facilitated if we focus on their progress and not on the times they fail.

Errors to Be Avoided

Not only do we need to impart a positive moral influence to our adolescents, but we also need to avoid several common errors that inhibit moral development. Avoiding these errors frees a parent to concentrate on doing some of the productive things discussed in the final section of this chapter.

1. Underestimating the Problem

My young people occasionally say, "You know, Dad, this isn't going to be easy." At other times they say, "It might seem simple to you, but it is really hard for me." They sense that my optimism causes me to underestimate the problems that they as teenagers face in issues related to values and morals. Doing the right thing seems simple enough, but do you know what it is like being rejected by your peers (who see you as a square)? Do you know what it is like having your life threatened if you stand up against something that is wrong? I was shocked when I realized one of my teenagers was threatened in this way. Parents rarely grasp the pressures their adolescents face from others.

Discussions related to values and morals are difficult and effective parents must first recognize this. Second, they must communicate this realization to their teenager. There are times when you need to protect them. For example, at times when my daughter shares conflicts she is facing with me, I tell her I am willing to be "the heavy." I am willing to be the one who imposes restrictions on her if she needs to be able to say, "My parents won't let me." Saying, "My parents won't let me," is often an intermediate step before being able to say, "I don't want to," or "I don't believe that I should." I consider this a part of their growth, rather than a sign of weakness.

2. Overestimating the Problem

Have you ever tried to kill a mosquito with a 12-gauge shotgun? If your eyesight is good and you are close enough you will probably hit him. The problem is that you will do much other damage in the process. If you overestimate the problem of helping your child develop values, you cause overkill, which does more harm than good. Some parents do this when they try to protect their teenager from the frustration that goes along with developing values.

Berkowitz underscores this problem specifically as it relates to helping individuals come to value achievement.

> The "optimal challenge" requires occasional frustrations. If a task is to be sufficiently challenging the person obviously must have some hope of doing well. But he also must know that there is some chance he will fail, and he must have experienced occasional thwartings in the past if he is to believe that there really is some risk to the undertaking. Contrary to the theorist who believes in self-actualization, we may not be helping a person in the long run if we satisfy his every whim so that he never meets failures and frustrations.[8]

In order to avoid the pitfall of overestimating the problem your teenager faces in developing values, you must realize that you need to give him the right to fail. Otherwise, you will work so hard at being a "good" parent that you will end up not being an effective one. A good parent feels that he must fix everything for the teenager if he is to be considered worthwhile. There are many parents who are very effective who do not fix things for their children. They allow them to learn to fix things and develop values for themselves.

3. Taking Away Responsibility

Overestimating the problem often leads to the third error to be avoided, which is taking away responsibility and the opportunity to learn. Someone has said that children learn more quickly those things for which they take the most responsibility. We must come to value our teenagers too much to deny them the opportunity to learn. Allow your teens to take responsibility for themselves and for the values they choose, for this is one of their greatest opportunities for growth. Growth is not produced by just telling them what to do and expecting them to do it. They need to try out their values to see if they work.

If you want to test your maturity in this area, allow one of your teenagers to plan a party at your house for his peers. Don't be surprised at the internal struggles this will create for you. Will you let your teenager wrestle with the values he wants to promote through the party? Will you let him worry about his own reputation as well as God's and yours? If you care sufficiently about the issues they need to consider, you will be amazed at the good decisions they make, once you allow them to be responsible.

4. Withdrawing from the Process

Some parents take too much responsibility away from their teenagers while others refuse to take any responsibility. I tend to withdraw when I do not feel that I have all the answers. In so doing, I take myself out of the arena where answers are found through dialogue with my teenagers. Obviously I can't help others to see clearly when I have sand in my eyes. I need to provide more guidance than that. I find that I usually do not have to have all the answers when I come to the arena, but I always must be willing to *come*. Otherwise all the input my teenagers get will be from teachers, friends, and other persons whom I often do not even know. Getting involved is scary at times, but in the long run staying on the sidelines is much more frightening.

5. Killing Your Right to Be Heard

Most teenagers are at least partially deaf. They cannot hear what their parents say. Unfortunately, this has a negative effect on the way in which they develop values. They hear input from others, but not from their parents. The best cure for this ailment is to communicate more by saying less. My teenagers do not hear when I yell, but they often hear when I whisper. They do not hear when I pontificate, but they hear when I ask questions.

There were two secrets to the successful communication of Jesus. He asked questions and He told stories which people were required to think about in order to understand. These techniques resulted in people constantly asking Him to explain what He believed. This, of course, is right where we want to be to help our teenagers acquire values. We want them to be asking questions. The hardest thing in the world for a parent to do is to stop talking in order to be heard. We kill our right to be heard by our excessive use of words, but unfortunately we just keep it up.

The following quotes show how teenagers look at the way their parents try to communicate.

Says Barry, age seventeen: "My mother does not converse, she lectures. She turns the simplest idea into a complex inquiry. I ask a short question, she gives me a long answer. I avoid her. Her speeches take too much of my time. I wish she talked in sentences and paragraphs, not in chapters."

Says Leroy, age eighteen: "My father is unable to feel close to people. His talk is never person to person, it is always station to station. He judges in advance. He categorizes and pigeon holes and remains a stranger even to us, his own children."

Says Bess, age sixteen: "My father is sensitive to temperature but not to temperament. He is totally unaware of emotions and moods. He does not read between the lines, and cannot sense words unsaid. He can talk at length without ever becoming aware that he has lost his audience. He does not see obvious signs of boredom. He never notices that he has lost an argument. He merely thinks he has failed to make his position clear. He talks but does not communicate. He teaches and pontificates, and runs any conversation into the ground."[9]

Excessive talk may be tolerated by our teenagers when we are sharing fishing stories or discussing an experience we have shared. But excessive talk becomes detrimental when we get into the areas where we seek to stimulate growth and the consideration of new ideas. One young man said, "You know, sometimes my dad just talks himself right out of the ball game. I start out wanting to listen but when he won't stop I just shut him off completely." Earn the right to be heard by talking less and letting your teenager enjoy it more.

6. Heaping on Guilt

"I don't intend to belittle my children," one mother said with tears in her eyes. "I just don't seem to know any better. Sometimes even when I am trying to encourage them, I seem to end up making them feel guilty." When parenting comes to values and morals, most of us are very fearful. We are afraid we will fail in this area and then our children won't turn out right. This fear causes us to heap guilt upon ourselves. The higher we pile guilt on ourselves, the greater the chance is that we will begin to slide that guilt over on our children.

If you wish to avoid doing this, you must seek to spend more time describing and less time evaluating. Gordon has pointed out that we often speak with a language of unacceptance. Some of the characteristics of that language are: ordering, warning, preaching, giving logical arguments, and name calling. Each aspect of this language results in guilt being heaped on the teenager whether we intend to do so or not. When you inadvertently heap guilt on your teenagers you are closing the door to effective communication and input in their lives. Seek to be open about your values without trying to force them to devalue who they are or what they believe.

Lest I heap guilt on the reader, I must point out that no one avoids all the pitfalls all the time. Become aware of them to open the option of doing things differently. If you are aware of the problem you have in a given area, you are able to change the way you relate to your teenager in that area. Set high standards for yourself, but do not allow your perfectionism to result in guilt. That guilt is just as debilitating for you as it is for your teenager.

The Goal We Seek

What are we seeking to do when we relate to our children in a positive way regarding morals and values? A number of years ago I decided that the best model for me to follow in this area was the model of the consultant. The consultant is one who is available to perform one or more of the following functions: He helps to solve a problem, helps to understand a situation, or helps to evaluate resources. I want to be available to my teenagers to do any or all of these tasks.

I am delighted when one of my teenagers says, "Dad, what do you think I should do about this?" The temptation is to play the expert and *give* them answers, instead of helping them *find* the answers for themselves. Without being evasive I need to ask, "What do you want to accomplish? Tell me more about the situation. What goals do you want to reach? What are your standards or values to which you want to be true?

A number of years after accepting the role of a values consultant I realized that at least one expert in the field (Thomas Gordon) was suggesting this as an appropriate role for teachers.[10] If it is important for teachers, it is no less important for parents.

By the time your children become teenagers you cannot impose your values on them—they won't buy what you are selling—and you dare not abandon the cause. The only alternative is to try to build a relationship with your teenager in such a way that they see you as someone who is helpful to consult in developing values. Gordon has specified some of the conditions we need to heed to be effective consultants.

The effective consultant works by four basic rules:

1. He does not start out trying to change the client until he is certain *he has been hired*.

2. He comes *adequately prepared* with facts, information, data.

3. He *shares his expertise* succinctly, briefly, and only once— he doesn't hassle.

4. He *leaves responsibility with the client* for accepting his efforts to effect change.[11]

Parents are somewhat different than teachers in that they have been appointed to the job by God. It is true, however, that they are not effective unless the adolescent has a feeling that he has also hired the parent to help in this role. This is Rule 1. Rules 2-4 will help you stay hired. Know what you are talking about, but don't overwhelm your teenager with facts. Be careful to correctly label opinions as opinions— not as facts. Be brief. Leave them with the feeling that you will help them even more if they figure out how to get you to do so. Let them feel responsible for themselves without feeling guilty if they don't take all the sage wisdom you share.

Being a consultant seems to be a thankless job with little value if you are used to having people totally dependent on you. However, the job is not thankless and it is not unimportant. It is the most wonderful job in the world. Even when you are not sure how to be the most helpful, God will honor your willingness to be available to the Holy Spirit as He does His job of instructing your teenager in the area of values.

Footnotes

[1]Norman T. Feather, "Values in Adolescence," *Handbook of Adolescent Psychology,* ed. Joseph Adelson (New York: Wiley-Interscience Publications, 1980), p. 281.

[2]James E Marcia, "Ego Identity Status: Relationship to Change in Self Esteem," *Journal of Personality* 35 (1967): 119.

[3]Leonard Berkowitz, *The Development of Motives and Values in the Child* (New York: Basic Books, Inc., 1964), pp. 55-56.

[4]I have discussed the pornography problem in detail in *The Business of Boredom,* published by InterVarsity Press.

[5]See Figure 7 in chapter 6. Also see chapter 3 of my book *Faith and Personality,* published by InterVarsity Press.

[6]Beth Sulzer-Azaroff and G. Roy Mayer, *Applying Behavior-Analysis Procedures with Children and Youth* (New York: Holt, Rinehart and Winston, 1977), p. 91.

[7]Rudolf Dreikurs and Loren Grey, *A New Approach to Discipline: Logical Consequences* (New York: Hawthorne Books, Inc., 1968), p. 56.

[8]Berkowitz, p. 43.

[9]Haim G. Ginott, *Between Parent and Teenager* (New York: Avon Books, 1969), pp. 41-42.

[10]See *Teacher Effectiveness Training* by Thomas Gordon (New York: David McKay Company, Inc., 1974).

[11]Gordon, p. 294.

Chapter 9

Helping Your Teen Become Autonomous

Turning loose is hard, Lord! How can I do it?

Autonomy has been defined by John Dacey in *Adolescents Today* as "Independence of thought and behavior; self-ruling."[1] This definition is frightening to most parents because there is something within us that yells, "No! I don't want them to be independent. I don't want them to think for themselves. I'm afraid of their behavior. I want to keep control. I don't want them to rule themselves."

There are other times, however, when as parents we realize just how important it is to produce young adults who are capable of being independent and of regulating themselves. Helping children move from a place of total dependence at birth to becoming independent or autonomous at age eighteen or twenty is not easy. It requires careful thought and courageous action.

One of the big difficulties in helping our young people grow up is caused by our own heavy investment in how they turn out. Thus we see them as another product, like a shirt we sew or a cupboard we build. In the process we lose sight of the fact that God has used us to give them the breath of life, but He has not withdrawn from His commitment to their well-being.

The Old Testament story of Samuel is very informative at this point. Hannah, Samuel's mother, gave her miracle child back to the Lord, just as she explained to Eli: *"I prayed for this child, and the LORD has granted me what I asked of him. So now I give him to the LORD. For his whole life he will be given over to the LORD' "* (1 Samuel 1:27-28).

Later in the book of Samuel we find that Hannah's decision was

honored by God, for *"the boy Samuel continued to grow in stature
and in favor with the LORD and with men"* (1 Samuel 2:26).

In 1 Samuel 3:19 we read: *"The LORD was with Samuel as he grew
up, and he let none of his words fall to the ground."* Sometimes I
would become very frightened for my children if not for the fact that
we have a trustworthy God who is drawing our teenagers to Himself
just as He has drawn us.

In order to be autonomous, the adolescent needs several things.
First, he needs physical and emotional maturity. Literally, he needs to
grow up. Second, he needs spiritual identity. The faith of his fathers
needs to become his own faith. Third, he needs an attitude of expectation. He needs to believe that he has what it takes to carry on with his
life. This is tied in with identity, which will be discussed in Chapter 10.
Many young people wait twenty years to become adults, only to find
out that they don't know how to be adults. When this happens, we as
parents have not done our job.

In the pages that follow we will look at five responsibilities that we
have as parents which, when completed, will result in our teenagers'
becoming healthy, autonomous adults.

1. Equip Them

On numerous occasions I have had older adolescents sit in my office
with tears streaming down their cheeks, frustrated because they don't
know how to live independently. Jim said it well, "I try to be myself,
but it never works out. I don't know how to be an adult. My parents did
everything for me and now they are gone. I feel really ripped off."

Watching a father patiently teach his son how to hit a baseball brings
back a flood of memories of the times my own dad spent with me.
Fathers often spend hours helping their children to acquire physical
skills. These skills are important, but certainly are not all there is to life.
There are many skills which must be learned before a person is ready
for autonomous living. These skills need to be taught if the young person is to be properly equipped.

I find it helpful to think of a personality in four basic components:
thinking, feeling, doing, and choosing. (These components were presented in Figure 6. Refer to this figure as you continue reading.)
Choice is placed in the center of these elements because, as adults, we
make choices which relate to each of the other components. We must
learn to live by faith in each of these four areas.[2] As parents, we must
also equip our teenagers to be autonomous in each area. Let's

examine them briefly on an individual basis.

. . . for Autonomous Thinking

How do you equip a young person to be autonomous in the *thinking* area? My parents equipped me by allowing me to think. They didn't give me all the answers. Sometimes they made me dig for them. "What do you think?" they asked. They listened to thousands of questions, but didn't feel compelled to provide all the answers. When adolescents are allowed to think for themselves, they develop confidence in their own ability to think. We need to encourage young people to think about all areas of life. There is a place for providing specific input, but that input is often best received after the young person is encouraged to think for himself. As I observe families of underachievers, I find that the parents of children who underachieve tend to do too much for the children and to provide too much direct input. Young people need to be forced to think through things on their own, including their faith. As they think through things on their own, the values, thoughts, and beliefs become theirs. Don't tell them what they think or believe. Ask them!

Intellectual growth is best fostered by quiet example and patience. We do not teach thinking by demonstrating our supposed intellectual superiority. When I wax eloquent with my teenagers, they often say, "We know, Dad! You have a brain!" The implication is clear. "Don't forget that we have brains, too!"

Equipping your teenager to think is not all passive. It doesn't just involve asking questions. There is a place for stating your point of view. Do so, however, in a manner which will enable your teenager to think about your views, rather than just having to swallow them whole.

Parents also need to be active in providing intellectual stimulation for their teenagers. Occasionally, give your teenager a *short* article or paragraph from a newspaper and ask him to read it. Remember to follow up on assignments which you give to him. Ask him what he thinks about the reading. You will be amazed when you see how bright he is. Also put your teenager in contact with good books and thinking people. He will welcome an alternative to the boredom of TV.

Young people sometimes resist your efforts to involve them in activities other than the usual ones such as sports, entertainment, or passive activities. Do not be sidetracked by this resistance. They, like us, will resist anything until they have a chance to try it. Approach intellectual pursuits in a serious, yet light, manner. Teach them that learning is fun. Don't recreate a bad school situation. It is helpful to ask yourself,

"Would I enjoy this if I were a teenager?" And then, if not, "How could I change the plan to make it more exciting?"

When children show interest in a specific intellectual area, help them to pursue that area. Help them to find books and other materials which will develop their intellectual experience on a given topic. This expertise will in turn help to improve their self-acceptance.

. . . for Autonomous Feelings

The second area of equipping is in the *feeling* area. To help our teenagers to become emotionally mature, we need to teach them how to express their feelings and how to take responsibility for them.

Swihart has pointed out that we do one of three things with our emotions. We express them (get them out), repress them, or confess them. *Expression* is either positive or negative. Acting out one's anger is a negative expression, while telling someone you are angry without striking them is positive. The important thing with expression is to get in touch with what we are feeling.

Emotional autonomy is aided by parents who allow their children to experience their emotions without telling them what to feel. The following example from Welter's book presents two responses to emotions in children.

> There are two eight-year-old girls, Barb and Doris, in an argument. They get so mad they hit each other, and then they both run home crying. Suppose you had x-ray vision and super hearing and could observe them running into their own houses and yelling the same sentence to their mothers: "Doris (Barb) hit me and I hate her!" The mother's reply:
> Barb's Mother: "Barb! You don't really hate her."
> Doris's Mother: "It really hurt to be hit, especially by such a good friend as Barb."[3]

Obviously, the response of Doris's mother will facilitate emotional awareness and growth, while the response of Barb's mother will only hinder Barb's awareness of her feelings.

Young people need to learn that emotions can be experienced, and experienced fully, without the need for negative expression. In the emotional area, doing what comes naturally is not always productive. When your teenager has been inappropriate emotionally, don't lash out at him or say what you would have done. Ask him how he would like to respond to his feelings. Answering this question will result in greater emotional maturity.

When you fail in terms of the way you react emotionally with your teenager, do not be afraid to admit your inappropriate expression of feelings. "I'm sorry I said you were stupid, Joe. I was frustrated because the yard wasn't mowed. You need to know I'm frustrated, but you also need to know I don't think you are stupid." This type of emotional regrouping needs to be practiced with your teens so that they, too, can learn to emotionally regroup. The ability to regroup emotionally is an important part of becoming autonomous.

Repression of feelings is particularly damaging because the young person does not understand his feelings. Swihart explains the damage repression causes.

> Repression comes at great cost for it saps our energies like a hidden short in an electrical system. It takes effort to keep these feelings hidden in the recesses of our unconscious. As a child, did you ever play with a bit of wood or a balloon, trying to push it under the surface of a tank of water? It was fun and fascinating because it was so difficult to keep it from floating to the surface. Keeping down feelings that we fear will blow up in our face or reveal us as some kind of monster is an energy drain that leaves us less able to help others and to be about the King's business in general.[4]

Getting feelings out in the open, without the crippling effect of negative expression, is a valuable tool to give to your children. Help your young person avoid repression by listening and identifying with the emotions expressed. Don't take them lightly or feel that you have to do something about them.

A part of becoming emotionally autonomous is to own your feelings and to decide how you want to act on those feelings. This is what Swihart calls *confession* of our feelings—owning them and taking responsibility for them. To take responsibility is to be able to say to yourself, "I may be really depressed, but I am not going to choose to withdraw from God or people. I need to respond to my depression by staying involved. I can make choices that are good for me."

. . . for Autonomous Doing

The next area of equipping your teenager is the area of *doing*. Help him to learn the skills of life whether physical, social, or survival. The most effective parents are those who lead their young people to learn new things without forcing them. Doing skills are best learned by doing *with*. Modeling is the best way to teach. This is true if you want to teach your son to cook or if you want to help your daughter to learn to tune the family car. Do *with* them.

In the area of social skills, children need to be able to watch you carefully. For example, how will they learn how to apologize if they never see you apologize? How will they learn how to treat a lady if they don't see you treat your wife in this manner? The more things you do with your young person, the better teacher you become.

Giving them the opportunity to learn to do from others is also helpful. They will feel less pressure. My son loves to work with his grandfather, because he sees how things are done and he also gets better acquainted in the process. If you don't sail, but your son or daughter would like to learn, you might trade them for a weekend for the teenagers of a friend who sails all the time. Your friend's teenagers will learn how to camp or garden with you in the process.

Don't just assume that your teenagers know how to do everything. Observe, and where you see inability make the opportunity to learn available if possible. Keep in mind that they have to be ready to learn. You cannot force your interests on them. Your job is to make the learning opportunities available.

. . . for Autonomous Choosing

The fourth area of equipping is the area of *choosing*. Decision making is a definite skill that all persons need to learn if they are to be autonomous. Decision making is learned by making decisions. Parents need to begin early to train their children to choose. Choosing causes the young person to grapple with his world. When you are allowed to make choices, you soon realize that life is not always fair or easy.

Unfortunately, many parents make all the decisions, and their children grow up with a distorted picture of what life is like. Adolescents who learn how to weigh alternatives and to make commitments are more healthy mentally. They find accepting themselves easier, even after they have learned that they sometimes make poor decisions. The opportunity to fail is important as we progress towards autonomy.

In helping children to learn to make decisions, be cautious at first. Let them make choices within the safety of acceptable limits. You may not choose to allow your young son to decide whether or not he will wear trousers, but you can allow him to choose which pair of trousers to wear. Later on he will need to learn to choose which is most appropriate to wear—shorts or trousers—for a specific occasion. Most teenagers start choice training too late, and therefore when the adolescent begins to make many important decisions, he is ill prepared.

What is our goal then in equipping our teenagers? Our goal is human effectiveness. We want them to develop the skills we have, and more if possible.

2. Encourage Them

Teenagers have an exaggerated view of their parents. You may not realize it, but to them you are awesome. I know they are aware of your weaknesses, but you are still high on their list. One of the neat things to do for your teenagers is to point out the steps you see them taking toward being autonomous. Jill stated, "It makes me feel good when my parents recognize that I'm a person all by myself."

As you seek to encourage them, you will find that your teenagers will not always know how to accept the praise which you offer. Description is much more effective than evaluation. It is helpful to describe what they do that is good or effective, without glorifying them as persons. They know that too much unrealistic praise just sets them up for future failure.

Young people like to know that they are becoming adults in the positive sense. Phrases like, "You are handling that well," or "I have confidence in you," are helpful to them as they learn what standing on their own two feet means. Young people need reassurance, particularly in the social area. When asked direct questions, be sure to acknowledge that your judgments are based on the facts which you have. When my daughter Marcy asks for advice, I ask her to specify the details, and then to tell me what she has done or is planning to do. As I get the facts I ask, "Have you considered this?" or "What would happen if you did this?" As the facts are unraveled I encourage and praise her in those areas where I see her taking good steps. She appreciates my encouragement.

There is a second area of encouragement different from praise or positive reinforcement. This is encouraging young people toward autonomous action. Young people often need to be encouraged to act on their own behalf. Letting children set their own limits, or encouraging them to establish their own rules, are helpful steps toward autonomy. Initially, these decisions should be made in consultation with you as a parent. Keep in mind the importance of adolescents making decisions that they can live with. They are the ones that need to learn. You have had your turn.

Encouraging early teens to get involved in new experiences is also important. Once again, this is best done by doing *with* them. If you ask a teenager if they want to do something, the response will often be "No." This response often has nothing at all to do with the activity, but is related to the fear of the unknown. Encourage young people to learn skills and to go to new things, even if they are uncertain if they will like them or not. Each experience gives them a better base from which to decide what kind of person they wish to become.

3. Excite Them

Parents are often guilty of being so negative about life that teenagers justifiably dread growing up. The fatalism of the 1960s was due in part to the Vietnam war and other social problems, but it also reflected the negative attitudes of the parents of the flower children. If young people grow up feeling that life is absurd, they usually have been exposed to a heavy dose of absurdity from their parents.

Injecting your teenager with possibility thinking is important. Murphy's law—the belief that if anything bad can happen, it will—needs to be challenged. It is true that bad things do happen in a sinful world, but it is not true that all we have to look forward to is negative—negative—negative. Christianity is indeed a positive faith, a faith of hope and good things, flowing from the goodness of God. Dare we teach our teenager anything less?

All good advice needs to be carefully balanced with a caution, and the challenge to be enthusiastic is no exception. Some parents make the mistake of using excitement as a hook. Don't use your excitement about the talents of your teenagers as a means of prodding them on to new activities; rather, recognize their talents as a possible point of contact. Teenagers resist attempts to excite them about things that their parents want, rather than what they need. One young man said, "I'm sick and tired of my dad trying to create me in his image." Remember: this chapter is about helping your young people become autonomous—not about exciting them about your dreams for them.

By definition, autonomy is different from fitting into someone else's mold. Autonomy is independence of thought and behavior. As a parent, I like my way of life, my Christian values, and my work. But I must resist the temptation to feel that my work is not done unless my children all walk the same paths. Sometimes they find a better way.

In a letter to a friend, seventeen-year-old Harold wrote: "When I look at adults, I see greed and ambition. All they want out of life is a big bank account, a house in the country, two cars and a yacht. . . . Is my father happy? No. He is miserable. He is overworked and worn out. He is pressed by time and taxes. He is tormented by headaches and doubts. . . . At his pinnacle of prominence, he is a bent and spent old man. I refuse to be like my father. I do not want to amass fortunes, or pile up posses- sions. I am sick of such 'successes.' I am determined to avoid the rat race.[5]

Young people are excited when they are helped to discover who they are and what they can become. Excitement is, however, different from motivation by guilt. Help them to see possibilities in being self- governed without feeling pressure to do the impossible.

4. Emancipate Them

In the 1970s the rise of the Church of Scientology and the World Church created new interest in the cults. The "Moonies" remind us once again of the power of one human being or subculture to control the mind. We abhor such control, and are reminded of the devastating effects of such control as seen in the Manson murders and the mass suicides of Jonestown. What we do not always think about is that we, as parents, often exercise tremendous mind control over our own chil- dren.

As I talk to different psychologists, I repeatedly find that a high per- centage of their clients are persons who feel locked into their parents. They are separate from their parents but not emancipated. They still live and breathe the deep sighs of dependency. Parents need to take a more active role in setting them free. Jim is over thirty years of age and is still struggling to be successful, even though he has risen to a high management position in his company. His salary is excellent, his little family is great, and he is very excited about his church family. Why, then, is he so fearful and depressed?

As I explored this with him, the answer became clear. He is still try- ing to succeed for his parents' sake. He still lives with the message that he must be successful or his mom and dad will have somehow failed. His parents gave him the message that it was okay to win, but never the message that they still loved him when he was average. He is inde- pendent from his parents financially and geographically, but he is as much imprisoned to them as though he were still living back home.

Communicating a Sense of Emancipation

As I look back over my own childhood, I realize that my own parents somehow gave me a sense of being emancipated from them without leaving me feeling abandoned or insecure. I have tried to ferret out the elements of my childhood which helped me to become autonomous.

Some of my experiences are applicable to others as well.

First, *I felt deeply loved and appreciated for just being a round-headed little kid.* I didn't have to prove anything to my parents before they loved and accepted me. They loved me just the way I was.

Second, *my parents didn't always try to rescue me from the situation.* They let me fight my own battles, but I knew they were there for support.

Third, *they let me know that I couldn't always count on them to bail me out.* One of the greatest lessons I learned was that I could live without going to a school assembly. My dad and mom wanted me to go, but they didn't have a dime for the admission fee. They didn't make a big deal out of the situation one way or the other, but I experienced not being able to do everything others were doing. I value this lesson now.

Fourth, *they didn't always tell me what to do.* Some of my greatest lessons were learned on my own and then reaffirmed by my parents as we talked later.

Fifth, *my parents talked of the day when I would be on my own.* My dad did this especially. He created an anticipation of being autonomous. I didn't feel a bit dejected when Dad said, "When you get married, I want you to get far enough away from us, and far enough away from Sandy's parents, that we won't be meddling in your life. You two need to learn to deal with life together." Even before he was a believer, Dad was giving biblical advice. I found the principle he was using nestled neatly in Genesis 2:24: *"For this reason a man will leave his father and mother and be united to his wife, and they will become one flesh."*

When children are young, they constantly ask their parents for permission to do things or go places. Young people enter the teen years with a desire to make these decisions for themselves, but they still sense the need to have their parents' approval. One young lady said, "I want to do what I want, but with Mom and Dad's approval." To emancipate is to communicate to your teenager that he has not only the right to decide for himself, but also the responsibility to make that decision.

Too often parents only give control to the teenager when they don't know what else to do. It isn't very flattering for the teenager when you only give him autonomy when the situation is helpless and getting worse. Imagine being put into a ball game when your team is behind twenty points with two minutes to play. The coach lets you call all your own plays, but you aren't autonomous when you can't affect the outcome of the game.

Making a Declaration of Independence

I believe that in one way or another, young people need to receive a declaration of independence from their parents. In some cases this should be written or spoken. In all cases, it should be at least implied. Parents need to be deliberate in removing the hooks that they have used to control their young people. When the hooks are removed, then the adolescent is free to explore new ways to love and communicate with the parents, adult-to-adult. If you are unaware of some of the ways you are hooking your child, you need to talk to him, or his friends, or some of your friends who can help you to understand your relationship more fully. In some cases a couple of parent-teen emancipation sessions with a professional counselor are a good investment for future relationships.

5. Escape Them

Let's look at the other side of the coin now. Not only do we need to free our children, but we also need to pull free from them. The empty nest syndrome results in parents' feeling less worthy, because many of the things they used to do are no longer there to do. Rather than seeking to discover new outlets, some parents have remained available to their children, and have been used by their children. One mother said, "I don't have much to do now that the boys are gone, but I do resent being used as a washer woman."

Parents need to escape the demands of their young people to allow them to experience true autonomy. This escape needs to begin early in the life of the child. Don't do things for children which they are capable of doing for themselves. They resent you for this, and at the same time their self-acceptance suffers. Children who are pampered act out of line. Children who are helped to become independent are more relaxed.

I worked with a young family who had two boys, ages three and five. When the mother first came in she said that two days earlier the younger son had repeatedly bitten the older son. The mother was understandably frightened. When I quizzed her, I found that the incident was triggered by the older child trying to help (force) the younger to change his clothes. I also learned that the mother usually picked out all the clothes and dressed the boy. He had no sense of being able to do anything for himself. When he started to do something for himself, he cried until his mother rescued him. He was dependent and didn't feel good about himself as a result.

I advised her to tell him that it was now time for him to learn to do things for himself, and that she would no longer be dressing him. He resisted the first morning and cried for about an hour. The mother plugged her ears and prayed. All that time she was asking herself what this crazy psychologist had gotten her into. By noon the boy was dressed and had half a smile on his face. The mother straightened his shirt and praised him for his efforts.

The next morning there was no crying and the lad was dressed in time to go play with his friend. This time he wore a full smile. The mother reported that the biting (which had been going on for months) had now all but disappeared. The child had learned a valuable lesson which was a building block for future autonomous living and greater self-esteem. The mother was also beginning to learn that relaxing and not working so hard at mothering was okay.

The adverse effect that dependency has in young children is exaggerated even more if the dependency is continued into the teen years. Although the adolescent works to maintain dependency at the same time he is reaching for independence, the effects of dependency are still negative. Dependence creates resentment and hostility which destroys the parent-teen relationship.

In order to be increasingly dispensable to your teenagers, you need to learn to have your own needs met in ways other than doing things for them. The temptation to act for your teenager is seductive because as Christians we place a heavy emphasis on doing for others. The ultimate result of such doing, however, may be quite negative. Even when your teenager puts pressure on you to act for him, care should be taken to escape the trap and help him to develop the skills necessary for him to be autonomous.

Focus on the Goal

The five responsibilities which have been discussed are not ends in themselves, but are necessary steps to take if parents are to reach the goal of producing young adults who are capable of standing on their own two feet. We shudder when we read stories of persons who have been treated like children all their lives. I was appalled to hear of a thirty-year-old man who was still being fed by his mother and father, even though he was capable of caring for himself. Keeping a teenager dependent isn't much different.

Earlier we emphasized that parents have trouble turning loose because of feelings that their work isn't finished. We are fearful that we will take them out of the oven when they are only half-baked. The error, however, is usually in the other direction. We keep them in the oven until they are burned. There are definite dangers in seeing our children as products. We become anxious because we are fearful they will not be good products.

Most parents have accomplished much more with their children than they realize. I often see troubled parents who fail to realize what a good job they have done. If you want your teenager to be perfect, forget it. But if you want your teenager to be a decent, sound human being, relax and turn him loose. He will falter for a while like a person who has had a body cast removed, but in the long run he will learn to walk and to run on his own. John wrote: *"I have no greater joy than to hear that my children are walking in the truth"* (3 John 4). I believe that God intends that we experience this same joy with our teenagers. We must, however, keep the focus upon their walking alone. We cannot do the walking for them.

Footnotes

[1]John Stewart Dacey, *Adolescents Today* (Santa Monica: Goodyear Publishing Co., Inc., 1979), p. 419.
[2]See my book, *Faith and Personality* (published by InterVarsity Press) for a discussion of living by faith in the areas of thinking, feeling, doing, and choosing.
[3]Paul Welter, *Family Problems and Predicaments: How to Respond* (Wheaton, Ill.: Tyndale House Publishers, 1977), p. 42.
[4]Philip J. Swihart, *How to Live with Your Feelings* (Downers Grove, Ill.: InterVarsity Press, 1977), p. 19.
[5]Haim G. Ginott, *Between Parent and Teenager* (New York: Avon Books, 1969), pp. 129-130

Chapter 10

Helping Your Teen with Self-Acceptance

How can someone with so much to offer be so negative, God? I just don't understand!

Parents are often shocked when they realize that their teenagers suffer from a lack of self-acceptance. Parents see so much potential in their children, and value them so much, that it is hard for them to fathom the lack of self-worth they see exhibited by them. One mother said, "I just don't understand it! How could someone with so much to offer be so down on herself?" There is no getting around the fact that the lack of self-acceptance is a major problem for teenagers today. Is there anything that we as parents can do? I believe there are at least six ways we can help them.

1. Accept Yourself and Pass It On

The idea of being a chip off the old block runs deep in our minds. When we look at our parents we see many similarities. Some of these observations frighten us, while others make us glad. I am pleased that I have a bit of humor which I got from my father. I like it in him and I like it in me. I also realize that I am determined like my mother. She accomplished much because she hung in there. I like that in her and I like it when I see it in me.

I also realize that I have some negative qualities which my parents passed along. When I see those negative qualities, I am forced to evaluate myself. Can I accept myself if I have negative points? Am I willing to try to change those things I don't like? Can I be optimistic, or am I a fatalist? How I answer these questions will determine to a large part what I have to give to my teenagers to help them with self-acceptance.

Accepting the Good, the Bad, and the Ugly

Self-acceptance begins by telling it like it is. You and I each have strengths and weaknesses, just as everyone else has strengths and weaknesses. This is the bottom line. I must acknowledge who I am right now, strengths as well as weaknesses, before I accept myself enough to decide who and what I want to be.

The amount of emotional energy expended in hiding those negative things that we observe in ourselves is astounding. Imagine how powerful you would be if the energies wasted on covering up were spent in more productive ways. One person stated, "I spend about ninety percent of my energies just trying to keep secrets about myself." Eugene Kennedy explains how this keeps us from self-acceptance and honest self-expression.

> One of the troubles with living this way—aside from the amount of energy it demands—is that it kills our freedom and spontaneity, two of the most important qualities needed for a healthy attitude toward ourselves. We cannot be free when we are bound by the expectations of other people, when being ourselves might meet with disapproval and social failure. We make ourselves miserable when we live as though we were trying to avoid being blackballed at our favorite club. There is not much room left for ourselves—or for even finding out who we are—when impressing others becomes our basic style in life.[1]

Accepted in God's Sight

Self-acceptance also begins by acknowledging that God has made us as unique persons of worth. We have been damaged by sin, but we are valuable enough to be refurbished by God. I often view God as an antique dealer who delights in taking marred pieces and restoring them to a beautiful condition. God chooses to use our weaknesses, so we need not devalue them.

Many people who struggle with self-acceptance want to be different, but they do not know what they expect of themselves. This causes them to wallow in self-pity, rather than to trust God for the changes they desire. If you are stuck at this point, I suggest that you take the risk of setting some goals for yourself. How would you like to change? What characteristics would you like to see growing in your life? Going through this process yourself will give you the confidence you need to guide your teenagers into their process of personal growth. Coaches who have played the game usually have more credibility with their players.

What does accepting yourself as a parent mean? For me, this means *I am not perfect, but I am complete in Christ. God is enabling me and equipping me to be all He intends me to be. I will make mistakes but I will learn. I can change in those areas where change is needed. God and I are enough. I do not have to wait for another miracle before I begin to live.* Internalizing these statements is the heart of self-acceptance. Ask God to help you to say them and to believe them.

Communicating Acceptance to Your Teen

There are other statements that you, as a parent, need to make if you are to help your teenager develop self-acceptance. The statements are these: *I do not expect my children to complete me. They cannot do for me what I could not do for myself. I will enjoy them as people, rather than subtly demanding that they become all the things that I have not become.*

Failure to free your teenager and yourself from the tyranny of living your life through them will result in your love for them being seen as conditional and, subsequently, invalid. If you were frustrated because you did not finish college, rejoicing in your children's academics is fine, but you need to be able to accept the fact that they may choose not to go to college. Otherwise, the pressure you put on them will be so great that they will have trouble valuing themselves.

2. Be Positive—Challenge Your Teen's Negative Evaluations

Modern Christianity has somehow preached the myth that being negative is a virtue. We have been led to believe that if we run ourselves down, we are more spiritual. Paul didn't believe this! He wrote that, *"Each one should test his own actions. Then he can take pride in himself, without comparing himself to somebody else, for each one should carry his own load."* (Galatians 6:4-5). We have fostered a type of false humility which believes that seeing ourselves as bad is beautiful. I am not in favor of self-worship or any other form of idolatry, but neither am I in favor of mislabeling ourselves in order to try to gain favor with God or man. When God created us, *"God saw all that he had made, and it was very good"* (Genesis 1:31a). Sin marred God's creation, but the work of Christ is to restore us to a place of wholeness, which is also good. I am convinced that God takes no pleasure in our efforts to depreciate what He has chosen to appreciate. Don't glamorize yourself, but at the same time don't call "junk" what God calls "good." Be realistic. Talk about the things you do well, and the things you cannot do, or need to learn to do. Recognize areas of victory and strive to conquer areas of defeat.

If you stop for a moment, you will realize that the people you enjoy most in life are the positive people—those individuals who help you smell the roses rather than complain about the thorns. When you are positive, you will have a positive impact on your teenagers. They don't need someone to teach them how to be negative. There are plenty of models for that. They need God's view, which is filled with hope and expectation. Our music teacher, Anita, has helped our children believe in themselves. She focuses on potential and progress, not on the mistakes. They value what she has taught them to do. Try being positive for a whole day. You will feel better at the day's end and you will see the difference reflected on the faces of your children. Don't be surprised if they ask you what is wrong.

Don't Crumble the Cake

One aspect of being positive is what my friend, Daryl, calls "not making crumbs." We sometimes have an uncanny knack of taking something good or beautiful and reducing it to crumbs. Here is a simple test of your crumb-making ability. What do you say when someone pays you a compliment? Do you say, "Oh, it's nothing"? Do you say, "I'm really not that good"? Or maybe you even say, "I didn't do it! God did!" All of these statements are making crumbs. You have taken your piece of cake, a compliment, and crumbled it. Even the statement about God is not accurate. God did not do it. He enabled you to do it. Be thankful to Him, but also be thankful to the person who gave you the piece of cake. The most appropriate response to a compliment that I have discovered is a simple "Thank you"—thank you to the person and thank you to God.

When Moses tried to make crumbs of himself before God by saying, *"Who am I?"* (Exodus 3:11), God continued with the piece of cake: *"And God said, 'I will be with you. And this will be the sign to you that it is I who have sent you: When you have brought the people out of Egypt, you will worship God on this mountain' "* (Exodus 3:12).

Moses continued to make crumbs until finally God lost patience and got another person, Aaron, to help with the job. Even then God continued to affirm Moses. Notice carefully the interaction recorded below.

*But Moses said, "O Lord, please send someone else to do it."
Then the* LORD's *anger burned against Moses and he said,
"What about your brother, Aaron the Levite? I know he can
speak well. He is already on his way to meet you, and his heart
will be glad when he sees you. You shall speak to him and put
words in his mouth; I will help both of you speak and will teach
you what to do. He will speak to the people for you, and it will be
as if he were your mouth and as if you were God to him. But take
this staff in your hand so you can perform miraculous signs with
it"* (Exodus 4:13-17).

If you are a crumb-maker, you need to learn to affirm yourself as well
as your teenager. Being objectively positive about yourself is difficult at
first, but it is the essence of self-acceptance.

Emphasize the Positive

A second aspect of being positive is helping your teenagers to view
themselves positively. Remember, being negative is never a virtue.
Young people sometimes develop the bad habit of labeling themselves negatively. You have heard them say, "I'm dumb. I'm ugly and
no one could ever like me." These bad habits begin because they want
you to challenge them. If you challenge these untrue statements,
young people will not believe them either. If allowed to persist, however, they will become a bad habit which will significantly affect the
adolescent's self-worth.

One way to challenge such statements is to ask, "Is that true?" Try to
challenge the person to make a more truthful statement. My daughter
sometimes says, "I'm so dumb," when she embarrasses herself. When
asked to make a more truthful statement, she says, "I'm embarrassed.
I wish I hadn't done that." You can do something about behavior
which embarrasses you. But there is little to be done for a person who
is dumb. Help your young person to make statements which leave
open the option of correcting behavior, rather than of merely labeling
himself as bad. Jesus never forced people to say over and over again
how sinful they were. He had them identify their sin and then told
them to *"go now and leave your life of sin"* (John 8:11b).

When your teenager is making negative self-statements, acknowledge how he feels, but challenge him to put those feelings into a more
positive framework. For example, when my son was degrading himself for failing to win a race, I asked, "What did you like about what you
did?" He smiled as he said, "Well, I did run my best time ever." "Let's
go celebrate then," I said. "It isn't every day you run your best time

ever."

Encourage your teenagers to give themselves positive labels rather than negative ones. Unfortunately, negative labeling permeates the teen culture, so your job isn't easy. Don't nag, but do be persistent. Find a positive way to be negative about negativism. Ask, "Is that true?" Then challenge the person to make a more truthful statement. As you put this into practice you will find that your teenagers will also help you to dispute the negative labels you put on yourself. Too often parents of teenagers experience the pain of hurting each other. Learning to help each other for a change is a real treat.

3. Examine Your Love Life with Your Teenager

"Most people do not ask for very much from life. To feel alive they must feel loved. They must sense that somebody else notices and makes room for them, that they measure up in the eyes of somebody else who likes them just as they are."[2] These words, written by Eugene Kennedy, focus on the need for learning how to love our teenagers. Notice the phrase, "to feel alive they must feel loved." Feeling love for someone isn't enough. That love must be communicated. It must be spoken and it must be demonstrated. If love is only spoken, and never demonstrated, it will seem hollow or won't be believed. If love is shown, but never spoken, it won't be recognized. Wise parents combine words with demonstration. With our children, as well as with our spouse, we need to learn to speak the language of love.

Communicate with Unconditional Love

The most common problem I observe in parent-teen love is conditionality. Love is not freely given as God intended, but is often held out as a carrot, to be given only when the teenager takes the necessary steps. In contrast, God's love cannot be earned. His love can only be received from He who freely gives. The same thing is true in parent-teen love. Your child cannot do enough to earn your love. You must choose to give love with no strings attached.

Too often we look to our teenagers for happiness. Inadvertently our expression of love for them becomes conditioned on what they do to make us happy. Rather than follow the so-called "Golden Rule" (see Matthew 7:12), we tend to distort the Scripture to read, "If you do unto me as I desire, I will do love unto you." This approach is clearly unsatisfactory.

As parents we contribute to the self-esteem of our adolescents by loving them unconditionally. Loving your adolescent is more than a feeling to be learned. Love is an action. Parents often ask me how they should contribute in love to their teenagers' self-esteem. "What should I be trying to communicate to them?" they ask. Bruce Narramore has specified four areas we should focus on to build self-acceptance in our teens. These are feelings of worth, competence, security, and love. As parents, we should have input in each of these areas. The chart presented below contrasts a positive and negative self-concept as viewed by Narramore.[3]

POSITIVE SELF-CONCEPT	NEGATIVE SELF-CONCEPT
Sense of Significance and Worth	Feeling of Badness and Worthlessness
Attitude of Confidence	Anxiety and Feelings of Inferiority
Feelings of Security	Insecurity and Worry
Awareness of Being Loved	Loneliness, Isolation, and Depression

Figure 10

Communicate a Sense of Significance and Worth

In order to communicate values as a person, the message of significance and worth must be shared. "You have value to me. I like to have you around. You are a neat person." This message is communicated nonverbally by being around the teenager, by spending time with him when you don't want anything from him.

Feelings of worth are often affected by the young person's perception of his physical appearance or mental abilities. How important is it for parents to help the adolescent in these areas? James Dobson has addressed the issue squarely.

> A parent who strongly opposes the unfortunate stress currently placed on beauty and brains, as I do, must resolve a difficult philosophical question with regard to his own children. While he recognizes the injustice of this value system, he knows his child is forced to compete in a world which worships those attributes. What should he do, then? Should he help his youngster

become as attractive as possible? Should he encourage his "average" child to excel in school? Or would he be wise to de-emphasize these values at home, hoping the child will learn to live with his handicaps?[4]

The answers to these questions are not easy. They require us to think about what our children value and the way in which they interpret their world.

Parents need to be aware that stylish clothes are viewed as symbols of worth. If you force your teenager to wear baggy hand-me-down pants and never let them try to be even a bit stylish, the teenager will feel a lack of worth from both you and his peers. Don't buy them everything they want, but do be sensitive to the need. What's good for the goose may not be good for the gosling.

Communicate an Attitude of Confidence

Confidence, or a feeling of competence, is communicated by helping the teenager to learn new tasks. This is best accomplished by doing with them, and is hindered by doing for them. Don't consistently do things for your teens that they are able to do for themselves. Help your adolescent acquire skills, and acknowledge the skills which he has acquired.

One caution is in order. You need to strike a balance between the skills you feel are important, and the skills that are valued by your teenager. Being competent in some things is important for the teenager (such as the Rubik's Cube), because these competencies help him to be accepted by his peers. Other competencies are important because they open doors for future opportunities. Knowing how to cook is an important competency for young men as well as young women. My son made cookies for his rough and tumble friends. They were amazed and their comments made him feel great. "Wow, Mike! I wish I could make something this good!" Children should be given the opportunity to learn basic skills.

Many young people, however, have been damaged by the fact that competence in sports has been given such a high priority in our society. If a child shows some ability and interest he should be encouraged but never pressured. You will live whether your son or daughter becomes a basketball star or not. If you develop an attitude of balance, they will feel less pressure and will find an aptitude level of expression of their interests. If they choose not to compete, encourage them to become competent at other things which spark their interest. Our oldest son shows some ability in wrestling (which I love), but has repeatedly said "No" when coaches have asked him to participate. He has found his area of competence to be hunting and fishing, which he loves. He has become a self-taught expert on deer and gets much positive attention because of this.

Teenagers need help in developing social competence as well. Help them to see what they do well. They are struggling. Let them know when you see progress. When they fail, listen, and then ask if they want suggestions. Don't tell them what to do unless they want your advice. Most of all, encourage them to try new things. They will find their niche if you support their efforts.

Communicating security is vital if your teenager is to develop self-acceptance. A twenty-seven-year-old student said, "I have lived in constant fear of being abandoned by my parents." We need to communicate that, while we do not like everything our teenagers do, we will not forsake them. We are going to make it together! Security is so basic to human behavior that the Bible stresses over and over again the security we have with God, our Heavenly Father.

Who shall separate us from the love of Christ? Shall trouble or hardship or persecution or famine or nakedness or danger or sword? As it is written: "For your sake we face death all day long; we are considered as sheep to be slaughtered." No, in all these things we are more than conquerors through him who loved us. For I am convinced that neither death nor life, neither angels nor demons, neither the present nor the future, nor any powers, neither height nor depth, nor anything else in all creation, will be able to separate us from the love of God that is in Christ Jesus our Lord (Romans 8:35-39).

Although we, as parents, cannot be as God to our teenagers, we need to stress the security factor with them, just as God has stressed it with us (see Deuteronomy 31:6).

Communicate Feelings of Security

Security is communicated nonverbally by simply being with the adolescent. I don't mean following him around. I mean spending time together at the breakfast table, or sitting on the edge of the bed—time to dry tears, or time to listen as anger is vented. The adolescent years have been described as the roller coaster years. To communicate security, you need to be willing to buckle in and ride the roller coaster of your adolescent's emotions.

Communicate Love

We emphasized communication of love earlier, but it needs to be underscored here because of its great importance. When young people are asked, "How do you know your parents love you?" the most common answer is, "They listen to me and they do a lot of things for me (provide for me)." Express your love in words ("I love you"), gestures (hugs), and in deeds (listening or being there). This is especially important during periods of conflict. Young people need to know that a disagreement does not mean that love has been withdrawn.

Parents also need to remember this: When your teenager resists or struggles against you, this does not mean that he doesn't love you. Don't use love as a tool of blackmail. Love is too important. Don't tell your child, "If you really loved me, you would do such and such." That is not a true statement. Keep the channel of love open even when areas of disagreement cause static.

4. Help Your Teenager to Acquire His Own Identity

In one sense, helping another person acquire his identity is impossible. Identity is not something you acquire. You have it whether you recognize it or not. Until you know who you are, however, you don't feel like anyone or anything. Dr. William Glasser has stressed the importance of the family in providing a base for identity development. He writes: "Because more families are breaking up than ever before, the family may seem more dispensable than it was in the past. The contrary is true. Until another institution can provide a role for children—and none, including the kibbutz, is in sight—the family continues to be indispensable."[5]

Accepting All I Am

In trying to help numerous adolescents answer the question, "Who am I?" I have come to recognize that the question is wrong. They aren't asking, "Who am I?" They want to know, "How can I be all the contradictory things I feel? I'm confused because it doesn't seem like all these things should be going on inside me."

Noted psychologist Dr. Erik Erikson has emphasized that the process of finding one's identity is a lifelong one, but the adolescent years are particularly crucial. During adolescence the struggle becomes the most intense. He writes: "In adolescence, for example, a compulsive person may attempt to free himself with maneuvers expressing the wish to 'get away with' things and yet find himself unable to get away even with the wish. For while such a young person learns evasion from others, his precocious conscience does not let him really get away with anything, and he goes through his identity crisis habitually ashamed, apologetic, and afraid to be seen; or else, in an 'overcompensatory' manner, he evinces a defiant kind of autonomy which may find sanction and ritual in the shameless defiance of gangs."[6]

I have found it helpful to remind adolescents, as well as myself, that they are all the things they think and feel. Until you accept what is there, you cannot exercise the option of choosing who you want to be. A part of developing self-acceptance is asking the optimistic question, "Who do I want to be?" rather than the fatalistic question, "Who am I?" One of the greatest gifts a parent gives to a teenager is helping him exercise choices which will free him to be who he chooses to be. You cannot teach this by telling alone. The teenager needs to be led to discover it.

Elizabeth, age eighteen, is struggling to find out who she is. She knows she is pretty, although sometimes she feels ugly. She knows she is not stupid, although she has begun to fail some of the classes she needs for high school graduation. She wants to be competent and independent, although she leans heavily on others and often doesn't do things she knows she is capable of doing. She has become lethargic and lives for pleasure, which she doesn't seem to be able to find.

I asked Elizabeth what it would take for her to take charge of her life. The concept was a struggle at first, but after a while she caught on. "When I refuse to get up in the morning, I let the system take charge of me," she observed. "When I stay in bed, I don't have the freedom to graduate. I am giving that control to the system." I helped Elizabeth to identify some things she wanted, and then to take the responsibility for going after them. It was obvious to her that other people were not going to deliver her wishes to her. Two months later she was back in school and passing her courses. "I've blown it a couple of times," she said, "but I'm doing better." It was obvious to me that she liked herself much better now than when I first saw her. She spoke less of being bored and showed more excitement about living her life.

Dealing with Boredom

Boredom is often a sign that the adolescent is not taking charge of his life. Elizabeth had to be helped to realize that boredom is a phase you go through in the process of being who you want to be. Regarding boredom, Paul Hauck has written: "What [some don't] seem to realize [is] that boredom is part and parcel to any endeavor that is undertaken. Whether it be listening to great music, eating wonderful food, making love, skiing, or whatever, it is impossible to do anything that one ordinarily enjoys without sometimes becoming bored. Woe to the man who cannot tolerate some boredom, for he shall forever be bored."[7]

The person who avoids activities because of potential boredom rarely finds satisfaction in anything. He spends so much time worrying about being bored that there is no time for enjoying the good things in life.

Rather than accept boredom as a fact, parents need to challenge the impulses of their teens and help them to work through it. I recently overheard an interaction between my wife and daughter, which shows one way of doing this.

Marcy: Mom, this day is awful! I'm bored!

Mom: Me too! Let's go to work and get it done so we aren't bored all day.

Discovering One's True Identity

There are five important steps to take in helping your teenager find his identity.

1. *Identify skills, interests, and opportunities.* Once again this is best accomplished by asking questions. "What do you like to do? What things do you do best? Do you think you could use this skill or interest in a vocation?" When parents ask these questions, teenagers often ask, "What do you think?" The parent is then free to share opinions without being seen as someone who lectures.

2. *Reaffirm or establish values.* Children or early adolescents often ask the question, "Mom, what do *we* believe?" When children are young, it is important to provide input by answering this question. As children mature, the question needs to be put back upon them. "What do *you* believe?" Ask questions such as, "How do you feel we should handle this? What do you feel is right?" Make the teenager struggle with the issue. Too often we end up arguing when we should be teaching.

We have found that when we engage our children in two-way conversation regarding what they believe, they are open to us and often ask us questions about our beliefs. This is reassuring, as this is one of the areas in which we hope to make an impact with them. We are not hesitant to say what we believe and why. If our values weren't worth holding we would abandon them. Your children do not want you to abandon your values. They want you to affirm them without ramming them down their throats. Give them time to think things through for themselves.

3. *Take responsibility for one's behavior.* Parents assist in this by keeping the focus on what the teenager does and the consequences of those actions (both negative and positive). Asking "What?" and "Was this what you wanted?" is more helpful than asking, "Why?" Our goal is not to ask our teenagers to defend themselves, but rather to evaluate their behavior and understand for themselves what they have been doing.

I received a call from the teacher of one of my sons. She indicated that he was disrupting her class, not doing his work, and was in danger of failing. (Just the kind of call a parent loves to get!) When I talked to my son, he told me how bad and unfair the teacher was and how much he hated the class. "That's fine," I said. "I accept those two things as facts. She is a bad teacher and you don't like the class. Now to my point. I expect you to stop disrupting the class and I expect you to pass."

He tried repeatedly to engage me in a discussion of the terribleness of the teacher but I stuck to my two points. "She is a bad teacher but you are not a bad student. You live up to your standards, not to hers." He fought me verbally for awhile and struggled with himself. He did take responsibility for his behavior, though, and was amazed and secretly proud when he got an A in the terrible class of the terrible teacher.

4. *Set goals.* Becoming is difficult if you don't know what you hope to become. When teenagers begin to see that they have abilities, discern some of the things they value, and take responsibility for their behavior, then goal setting is not nearly so frightening for them. Discussions of subjects like marriage, education, and vocation are difficult because of the modern society. Young people today need to have several options. They need to think through several choices and have their plans ready. This difficulty is often a blessing in disguise. Anxiety is a deterrent to boredom.

It is impossible for adolescents to assess their progress and thus know who they are becoming without some goals against which to measure themselves. Parents need to ask, "Where do you want to go? How will you know when you get there? What do you feel is the best course of action for you? Where do you want to be in five years?"

5. *Make choices consistent with the goals which have been set.* Par-

ents play an important part in this step as well. Remember, however, that you cannot make choices for your teenager. Simply encourage him to make choices. Allow the youngster to focus on the process of making choices, and don't place too much emphasis on the outcome. A teenager needs to be able to make his own mistakes. Don't criticize, but be supportive as he regroups and starts again. Acknowledge the good choices you see your teenager making. When he fails, don't rub it in. He feels bad enough already. All of us need to learn the importance of trying another way. This is a nonjudgmental way of saying, "If you don't succeed, choose again." Failure to reach your goal doesn't necessarily mean your choice was bad. It means that your choice wasn't effective. Blaming doesn't help, so why waste time?

Adolescents, like adults, suffer the consequences of overestimating their abilities and underestimating their obstacles. When this happens to your teenager, be available to talk it through. He may ask you for helpful suggestions. Help him to realize that making choices that don't work out is not a disgrace. Making choices is a much better way to live than letting others make all your choices for you.

Each of the factors stressed above contributes to the process of finding one's identity. Thinking about the process and what it means to your teenager is exciting.

5. Help Your Teenager to Find Worth Internally

Much of the time and emotional energy of the adolescent is spent in looking outside himself for some evidence of worth. The adolescent believes that if his friends say he is okay, then that is a fact. If they do not say he is okay, he must be rotten. This belief is dangerous because someone else is in control, telling you not only whether or not you have value, but also what you must do to acquire value. Many adolescents understand too late how damaging it is to have their self worth tied up in another person's appraisal. Sometimes this is learned from parents who offer only conditional love.

I have a friend who calls her mother each time she struggles with her self-acceptance. Each time her mother ends by saying things which make her feel much worse. She said, "I know better, but something inside of me just makes me want her approval so badly." Each time my friend seeks approval from her mother, she ends up disliking herself even more.

I believe that true self-acceptance comes from within. Self-acceptance comes from an awareness that God loves you and has made you okay. God's stamp of approval is clear and consistent. Note carefully what Paul writes in Romans 8:15b-17: *"And by him we cry, 'Abba, Father.' The Spirit himself testifies with our spirit that we are God's children. Now if we are children, then we are heirs—heirs of God and co-heirs with Christ, if indeed we share in his sufferings in order that we may also share in his glory."*

When a person receives Jesus Christ as Savior he is then indwelt by the Spirit of God, who becomes the internal source of validation. Teenagers need to be helped to realize that they validate their own worth by acknowledging the work of God in creating them and in enabling them to live a life of value. Even persons who are not believers cannot afford to look to people for self-acceptance. You cannot control people's reactions. You can, however, control yourself, and you can count on God, who stands ready to show acceptance to all who call upon Him. Romans 10:13 reads: *"Everyone who calls on the name of the Lord will be saved."*

6. Encourage the Life of Faith

The Scripture above leads us naturally into the final aspect of helping your teenager with self-acceptance. When an individual comes to realize that he has worth in God's sight, self-acceptance becomes a greater possibility. As the person learns to trust God and to find Him trustworthy, self-acceptance grows. Knowing intellectually and practically that God cares for you personally is exciting. As parents, we should help our teenagers become aware of just how much they are loved by God.

The way your teenager accepts himself is greatly affected by one additional factor. This factor is your acceptance of him. Don't be afraid to accept your teenager as a special gift from God. He will try your patience and test your faith, but he will also be a tremendous source of joy. Take the risk of complete acceptance. You will be the winner.

Footnotes

[1]Eugene Kennedy, *If You Really Knew Me Would You Still Like Me?* (Niles, Ill.: Argus Communications, 1975), p. 20.

[2]Kennedy, p. 10.

[3]Figure 10 is from Bruce Narramore, *You're Someone Special* (Grand Rapids, Mich.: Zondervan Publishing House, 1978), p. 133.

[4]James Dobson, *Hide or Seek* (Old Tappan, N.J.: Fleming H. Revell Co., 1974), pp. 76-77.

[5]William Glasser, *The Identity Society* (New York: Harper and Row, 1972), p. 103.

[6]Erik H. Erikson, *Identity, Youth and Crisis* (New York: W.W. Norton and Co., Inc., 1968), pp. 111-12.

[7]Paul A. Hauck, *How to Do What You Want to Do: The Art of Self Discipline* (Philadelphia: Westminster Press, 1976), pp. 28-29.

Chapter 11

Helping Your Teen Develop Responsibility

*I just wish that he would
follow through once, God!*

As we turned into our lane and rolled down the driveway, both my wife and I became very uneasy. We stopped the car just short of the garage and looked at each other. Our hunch had been correct. We had been promised that the lawn would be mowed by the time we returned home, and it clearly was not. The tall grass waved at us in the breeze as if to say, "I told you so." "But they promised," Sandy said. "I just wish that they would follow through once! It would do wonders to restore my confidence in the human race." These feelings that my wife expressed are echoed many times as we listen to parents at various seminars we have conducted. As parents we want desperately to have our children become responsible adults—even more responsible than we are.

A distraught parent brought a sixteen-year-old to see a famous pastor and Bible teacher. As the pastor talked to the parent and teenager, the picture became clear. The teen was not being responsible and the parent was seeing the matter as a spiritual problem. The pastor brought the matter into perspective by telling the parent, "I have never seen a spiritual sixteen-year-old." The young man's problem was not lack of trust in God, but lack of learning. He needed help in developing the ability to follow through on commitments.

As parents, we need to realize that most adolescents want to be responsible and they want to please us. The desire is there, but they don't put together a winning combination. There are so many things going on in their lives and in their minds that they get distracted and do

161

not follow through on the good intentions that they have. Possibly this is why the Scripture says, *"Train a child in the way he should go, and when he is old he will not turn from it"* (Proverbs 22:6). Perhaps not until later in life will the full impact of our training be realized in the life and behavior of the child. Adolescence is a period of life during which the activities and changes of life minimize the full effects of the training that we, as parents, have provided.

In the remainder of this chapter we will look at specific attitude traps which we, as parents, must avoid if we are to be successful. We will also examine several tools for teaching your teen how to be responsible.

Avoid the Attitude Traps

I do much better with my teenagers when I remind myself that being responsible is not natural. Responsibility is a social skill. Contrary to parental opinion, people survive without being responsible. All of us would agree, however, that learning responsibility is desirable and leads to a better quality of life for all who are involved. My younger son made his point by saying, "I'll bet when you were young, you didn't do everything you said you were going to do." I didn't say it to him, but I was startled by the thought. "I'll bet I don't follow through on everything even now," I realized.

1. *Expecting Responsible Behavior*

One of the biggest attitude traps is believing that your teenager *should* be responsible, even if you have not helped him to learn the behaviors that are a part of being responsible. If all teenagers were responsible that would be nice, but in reality they have to learn responsibility as you and I have had to learn it.

One of the things that helps me the most in allowing this learning to take place is to look at the progress, and not simply for the finished product. Young people become excited when they know that you see them progressing in some good directions. Tell them and tell yourself that God is at work in their lives, and that you like what you see happening. Teenagers are much more aware of their failures than we realize, and they are much less sure of their successes. One of the most effective ways to *"spur one another on toward love and good deeds"* (Hebrews 10:24) is to tell them when they have done a good job of being responsible. If being responsible were natural, this wouldn't be necessary, but remember, being responsible is not natural. It is hard work!

2. Taking Failures Personally

A second attitude trap is taking the failures of your teenagers personally. When you have been hurt or let down by a broken promise, it is easy to feel that the person hurt you on purpose. We erroneously believe that, "If they really love us, they will be responsible." Thus, when they are not responsible, we somehow believe that they do not love us or that they were trying to hurt us on purpose. This is not the case. The only thing that the irresponsibility of your adolescent proves is that he has not yet learned to be constantly responsible. This is the only point that needs your attention. If you believe anything else, you will set yourself up for further hurt because you will not be the kind of teacher that your adolescent needs to help him become more responsible.

One of the biggest mistakes parents make is focusing on the motives of the adolescent rather than focusing on the behaviors which would enable the teenager to act responsibly. In this regard, asking your teenager *what* rather than *why* is much more effective. Ask *what* they would have liked to have done, rather than *why* they didn't do it.

Asking *why* immediately puts the adolescent on the defensive. In truth they tell you that they do not know. This creates a real problem because you are not able to accept that answer, and you become defensive and push harder for an answer they cannot give. A power struggle develops and your relationship is seriously damaged.

I have found it helpful to respond to the lack of responsibility in my teenagers by saying something like, "I know you would like to be more responsible. Have you thought of anything that would help you in the future?" Wait and listen at this point. After you have heard them out, it may be appropriate to ask, "Is there anything I could do to help you?" They may not ask for help, but they value the fact that you cared enough to ask.

Avoid telling old war stories. Your adolescent is not helped when you tell how life was when you were a child. They are more interested in knowing that you care how life is for them now as they struggle to learn to be responsible. Marcy, my oldest, lovingly said, "Dad, that really isn't helpful! I'm not you! I'm me!" I realized that I was not telling her about my past struggles because it would help her, but because I was encouraged to realize that I had survived. *I* had become more responsible. Reminding your adolescents of growth you have seen in *them* is accepted as encouragement. Telling about how life has been for you is usually seen as unnecessary pressure.

3. *Expecting Perfection*

A third attitude trap is perfectionism. Before you overreact to the word, I must make it clear that I am not pushing mediocrity as opposed to perfection. I believe that we need to challenge our teenagers, as well as ourselves, to be all that we can be. But the attitude that refuses to acknowledge effort, but pushes for higher and higher levels of responsibility (without giving credit where credit is due) is damaging.

An illustration of this is conflicts that erupt over irresponsible time usage. Julie, age fourteen, is fifteen minutes late in starting to practice the flute. This upsets her mother and she interrupts Julie's practice session to tell her how upset she is with Julie's behavior. "You always start late," Mother comments. Julie opens her mouth to speak but Mother charges on. "I just wish that once you would be on time. You just aren't responsible. You never do what you know you are supposed to do."

By this time Julie no longer wants to talk to her mother. She is angry and just wishes Mother and her half-truths would go away. Mother misinterprets Julie's silence as obstinacy and screams at her, "Don't treat me that way! Who do you think you are?" Julie feels completely defeated. Mother finally leaves and Julie sits listlessly in front of her music stand. "Why should I practice?" she says to herself. "Mother never appreciates it, even when I do start on time."

If Marilyn, Julie's mother, had stopped to examine her perfectionistic attitude, this ugly scene could have been avoided. For one thing, Marilyn allowed her concern about Julie's tardiness to blot out her memory of Julie's typical practice behavior, which is quite consistent.

Perfectionism leads to faulty generalizations such as, "You always" or "You never." Teenagers know that such statements are not true and feel defeated when parents use them as clubs. If Mother had not been so perfectionistic she might have handled the situation in a better way. For example, when Julie had finished her practice, Mother might have said, "I noticed you got a late start tonight. Is it hard for you to put in your full hour every day?" Depending on Julie's response, Mother might encourage her even further by saying, "I've appreciated the fact that you have been able to keep such a heavy practice schedule. Most of the time you have been pretty consistent. Do you feel good about yourself when you use your time well?"

Responses such as these tend to emphasize acceptable performance and encourage the teenager to keep up the good work. When encouraged in this manner, a teenager usually strives even harder to meet the standards which have been set.

Playing the "Moving Target" Game

One of the most damaging things I have observed is what I call the "moving target" game. The game is initiated by a perfectionistic parent who directly, or indirectly, sends the message, "You will be acceptable when you show responsibility at this level." The adolescent responds by striving to please his parents, and often is right on target. The problem comes when the parent fails to acknowledge the responsible actions and then moves the target to an even higher level. The teenager says, "What's the use! I do what I think they want me to do and they are never satisfied. Sometimes I wonder if they even notice." This terrible game often causes the teenager to become angry and bitter. Parents are forbidden to play such games with their children (see Ephesians 6:4 and Colossians 3:21).

We are more effective as parents when we replace our perfectionistic attitudes with attitudes of appreciation and anticipation for the responsible behavior that our adolescent is developing. Parents often try to excuse themselves by saying, "But I'm only trying to help." Even though the statement may be true, the perfectionistic actions of the parents are usually anything but helpful. Note that teenagers who are driven by their parents' perfectionism usually do not develop an internalized standard of responsibility for themselves. This leads to feelings of inferiority or rebellion. Some teenagers say, "If I can't be good enough to satisfy you, I will show you just how bad I can be."

The standard of performance suggested by Paul Hauck seems to be a viable alternative to perfectionism. He emphasizes effort instead of achievement as a measure of success.

It is more important to do than to do well. The main difficulty people have who are driven by perfection is that they have a faulty definition of success. To them success is doing something 100 percent okay and hardly anything less. It simply does not make sense to define success as near-perfection. Think of success rather as a slight bit of improvement over what you were able to do before. Even if you are trying something and do not see improvement, you are still entitled to say that you are improving, because the benefits of practice will show up later. . . .
As long as you are attempting something, improvement is being made. Even if your performance goes down, as it sometimes will, you can still learn from the experience. And that is the name of the game.[1]

When you seek to help your adolescent develop responsibility, it is necessary to keep him interested in trying to learn responsibility. A perfectionistic attitude on the part of the parents is one of the hindrances to reaching this goal. Look for and reward progress. Don't demand perfection. Your teenager will be the first to point out that you don't even meet your own standard of perfection.

4. Devaluing Their Efforts

A fourth attitude trap which relates to perfectionism is devaluation. Devaluation refuses to see the full value of what the teenager does. Just as we are affected financially by devaluation of the dollar, adolescents are affected psychologically when we, as parents, devalue their efforts to be responsible.

I came home from work one evening and my son Mark said, "Dad, I fixed the window in the garage."

"Oh," I replied, "What was wrong?"

"I broke it."

"I don't know how many times I have told you to be more careful," I said, shaking my head in disgust.

As I walked away, I realized I had devalued both Mark and his efforts. I hadn't acknowledged his responsible behavior in repairing the broken window. He was hurt by my attitude, and I was hurting myself by choosing to focus on the negative factor, the broken window, instead of seizing the opportunity to enjoy with Mark the fact that he had developed both physically (he now had the skills to repair the window) and psychologically (he now had the maturity to see that he should repair things he breaks). Seeing the positive things your teenager does will help you avoid the trap of devaluing them. Even when their efforts turn out poorly, we need to recognize and value the fact that they made the effort.

A few years ago our family had the opportunity to go to Mexico. As we were swimming in the warm Pacific waters at Acapulco, I noticed a strong undertow and warned the children of the danger. A few minutes later a wave rolled me over and I landed on my head in about four feet of water. As I stood up I felt a tremendous blow to my left knee. I winced with the pain and became angry as I realized the source of the pain. Our younger son had dived and his head had smashed into my knee.

I yelled, "What do you think you are doing?!" I could see the hurt in his face as he said, "But Dad, I was trying to save you. I thought the wave was going to take you away." At that point I got control of myself and we sat down on the beach to enjoy a special moment of father-son affirmation. I initially devalued the results of his actions, but I was warmly pleased by his intentions.

5. Expressing Spite

Being spiteful is a fifth attitude trap that I have sometimes fallen into. I say to myself, "If they can't show responsibility to me, I won't be responsible to them." The results of this trap are chaotic. In my spiteful way I model the opposite of what I want my teenager to learn. This trap clearly leads to bad behavior as well as bad attitudes. Spiteful behavior always results in a power struggle between the adolescent and the parent. If he treats me poorly, I will treat him poorly in return. The more poorly I treat him, the worse I am treated. In fact, I get so involved in the process of trying to prove that I am right that I lose sight of my original objectives, which were to help my teenager to learn responsibility.

When you do unto your teenagers as they are doing unto you, you will not teach them responsibility. You will only anger them or, as Ephesians 6:4 states, *"exasperate"* them. My spiteful attitude has been helped by a determination on my part to meet my standards with my children whether or not they are being responsible. When dealing with childish attitudes, I do much better if I make a conscious effort to behave as an adult. Spitefulness has never proven to be helpful to me.

Steps to Facilitate Responsibility

We will now turn from the negatives to some positives. What are some specific things we can do to help our children become responsible?

1. Establishing Clear Standards

First, set clear standards which are obtainable by the adolescent. Parents often assume that their teenagers know what is expected without stating their standards. Adolescents are no better at mind reading than are their parents. Many times I assume that my teenagers have the same standards as I do and, therefore, if I ask them to do something, their performance will meet my standard. Wrong! They either choose to meet their own standard or to take the task lightly, thinking that if it were important a standard would have been set. If you want things to be done a specific way, then you need to give specific instructions. If it doesn't matter how things are done, as long as they are done, then you need not be specific. Disagreement over standards is often a wedge which gets driven deeply between teenagers and their parents.

Recently our son was asked to clean the kitchen before our company arrived. He did the cleaning and hurried back to watch the rest of a television program. His mother was not satisfied when she inspected the job. She called him back and told him to do it right. He did another quick job, but seemed satisfied that he had met his mother's standards. He had not, and when he was called back the third time he and his mother were angry.

As I observed the interaction, I saw several places where things broke down. First, he, like many teenagers, assumed he knew how to clean the kitchen, so he did not listen carefully to his mother's instructions. Somehow Sandy needed to get his attention. Second, Sandy assumed, on a couple of occasions, that he knew what she wanted and thus was not as specific as she could have been. Third, the greatest instructional tool of all, demonstration, was missing.

Showing is often better than telling. This is hard for parents since you can do the job in half the time it takes to demonstrate how to do it. The difference, however, is that if you *demonstrate,* the adolescent knows how to do it the next time. If you just *tell,* the outcome is uncertain. There is a great line in the book, *The Little Prince,* which states, "Words are the source of misunderstandings."[2] This is often the case when we talk about standards.

Although I often set standards, I fail to realize that the youngster may understand my standards, and yet still not be able to meet them. I realize this very vividly when I compare my abilities in fixing things with the abilities of my father-in-law, Howard. Howard is able to fix almost anything and he has often turned a near disaster into something neat. My wife Sandy grew up with Howard as a model of how adult males are able to fix things. Imagine how shocked she was to find that her husband has trouble fixing anything. For example, shortly after we were married I tried to fix a leaky faucet and ended up having to replace a broken sink.

Recently we solved the problem of standards. When she asks me to fix something, I ask her if she wants a "Howard job" or if an "Earl job" will do. If she wants a "Howard job," I either hire someone to do it or wait for Howard to visit. As the result of working with Howard, I have become more proficient, so occasionally I say, "I'm not sure I can do a 'Howard job,' but I'll try." With her support and encouragement a few of the jobs have come up to standard.

With teenagers it is important to let them know if we demand our standard or if their standard will do. If we demand our standard, doing the job with them is helpful. This alternative is superior to yelling at them, which produces guilt feelings for driving them away.

2. Specifying Selected Rules

When you are dealing with issues where rules rather than standards are the issue, then careful selection and specification of the rules is important. Even if your adolescents are good abstract thinkers, they will be very concrete about understanding rules if that meets their needs. At times they show little ability to predict the future. If rules are employed, they need to be carried out consistently and in a matter-of-fact manner. Don't waste time arguing over the rules. Be explicit enough about them that the youngster will know what to expect. This way if they choose to disobey they know what reaction to expect.

In enforcing rules to aid your teenager in becoming responsible, have a careful blend of law and grace. The law must be applied before grace is appreciated. However, as the Bible states, the law is harsh and at times we need to extend grace. Always remember that grace can be given or received, but it cannot be demanded. Your teenagers will not become responsible if they expect you to bend the rules. Choose rather to reward them for their efforts. My experience has taught me that periods of learning need to be balanced. My tightening of restrictions comes when the rules are not being taken seriously. Don't set more rules than you are prepared to enforce, since this will only cause you heartache. Rules should not be made to be broken. They should be made to be kept.

3. Setting Pre-determined Consequences

A third step toward responsibility is to set predetermined consequences (punishments, if you will), which are reasonable and related to the rule if possible. We like to have our thirteen-year-old son home for the evening meal. The family tries to eat at 6:00 P.M. Young people have trouble being punctual when they get heavily involved in what they are doing. Time passes quickly when you are having fun. But we have been firm with our rule. If you are not home by 6:00 P.M. sharp, you may not go to your friend's house after supper. This is not arguable. It is a fact.

Recently he came in late and before I could speak to him he said, "I know! I know! I blew it!" He felt bad enough without my giving him a verbal punishment. The consequences we had set were enough. On another occasion I chose to extend grace and let him go back as a reward for previous performance. Care needs to be taken so that the exceptions do not overshadow the rule. As far as rules are concerned, be factual, be consistent, and show enough love to encourage your teenager.

4. Using Logical Consequences

The use of logical consequences is valuable as a means of teaching responsibility. The term "logical consequences" refers specifically to allowing a teenager to experience the effects of his behavior in a natural (rather than an imposed) way. Spanking or grounding a teenager is not a logical consequence. Dreikurs and Grey give an example of the use of logical consequences to help teenagers learn to be responsible in cleaning up after themselves.

> My two teen-age daughters chose to leave the dishes for their mother. I left them until time for another meal. I prepared the meal in an untidy kitchen and announced the meal was ready. The girls found enough clean dishes to set the table. After the meal they took off and left the house and dishes in a mess. I left the house also and did not return until after suppertime. Everybody was home in a dirty mess with no meal and no mother. The girls reaped the consequence by washing the mess of dry, smelling dishes before a meal was prepared. They now say, "The sooner the dishes are washed, the better." This lesson is several years old, but remains fresh in their minds.[3]

One way to apply logical consequences is to allow teenagers to live with the results of their behavior. If they choose to sleep past breakfast time they will not get to eat until lunch. If they choose not to put their dirty clothes in the clothes hamper they will not get them washed. You don't have to make their choice and the results a big issue. That's just the way the situation is.

One of the most difficult areas in which we need to help teenagers become responsible is in the area of their use of time. Mothers often strive to please teenagers by having their meals ready for them on time, only to find that they do not allow enough time to eat. This is very discouraging for a mother and usually results in a conflict. A wise mother using logical consequences told her children she would no longer prepare meals since they were not eating them. It wasn't long before the youngsters requested that she resume her duties, and this time they arranged their time so that they could eat.

When logical consequences are applied, they focus on the adolescent's behavior, not on who is right. The teenager is given the right to choose. If he disregards the rule or the request, he must live with the consequences of that choice. People *do* become responsible when they are helped to recognize the relationship between their behavior and the events which follow. Parents are often too inclined to punish, but not inclined to let the adolescent learn in the way he learns best— by observing the consequences of his behavior. Punishment that is not related logically to consequences often produces side effects that damage the parent-teen relationship rather than strengthen it and teach responsibility.

5. Giving Positive Reinforcements

A fifth step to teaching responsibility is to apply positive reinforcement consistently when responsible behavior is demonstrated. A positive reinforcer is nothing more than a positive consequence following responsible behavior. It is a pat on the back, a special treat, or an appreciative word. Remember: Telling adolescents what they do right is more important than telling them what they do wrong.

Some parents are afraid that if they acknowledge the ways in which their adolescent is being responsible, those responsible behaviors will stop. That is not true. Behaviors which are followed by a positive acknowledgment or consequence tend to increase in frequency, while behaviors which are ignored or punished tend to decrease in frequency.

My experience has shown that young people long to have their parents acknowledge progress they are making. Try telling your teenager how much you see them growing to be responsible, and you will see his face light up. Be sure to wait until they have been responsible before you say anything. They know when you are being phony.

Some teenagers find taking positive reinforcement directly difficult. They get embarrassed, especially in front of their friends. Be creative. Write notes or even make a joke of it. Once, after my son had borrowed my tools and returned them without being reminded, I said, "How about that! You better be careful or I'll accuse you of being an adult!" He smiled, faked a scream, and said, "Oh no, I better put those back out in the rain."

When selecting positive reinforcers, keep in mind that what is positive for you may not be positive for your teenager. A kiss on the cheek may be a real reward for you, but it is a punishment for many teenage males. Rewards have to be matched to individuals. Otherwise they will not accomplish your objective. Social reinforcers are often the best— things like attention, kind words, smiles, compliments, or a gesture such as "thumbs up." You don't have to buy your teenager in order to positively reinforce responsible behavior.

6. Internalizing Standards

Some people are fearful about using positive reinforcement because they think such reinforcement will lead to externalized rather than internalized standards of responsibility. By externalized standards, we mean doing things for the reward rather than because they are good to do. Externalizing or internalizing has nothing to do with the rewards used, but is related to another step we need to take in order to teach responsibility. This step is helping the teenager to focus upon developing an internalized standard.

The method is simple but powerful. Rather than constantly telling the teenager how to be responsible in a given area, ask him what standard he would like to meet. For example, ask, "How would you like your room to look when the company comes?" or "What do you feel is a reasonable time for you to get in at night?" You will find that adolescents often come up with responsible standards. If they set the standards, they are much more likely to keep them. Your job as a parent is not to make your teenager responsible, but to help him to learn responsibility. This is often greatly facilitated by asking questions that lead the teenager to consider what he wants for himself.

Practicing between music lessons is often a source of conflict between parents and teenagers. Parents become policemen and teenagers become the convicts trying to escape. We grew weary of playing this policeman role with our piano player and decided to give the responsibility back to him. In doing this we tried to help him internalize a standard. We asked, "How do you want to feel about your piano playing?" He said, "I want to be ready so my teacher will be pleased." We then said, "You will have to work that out with her. We aren't going to tell you to practice or to time your practices. The piano lessons are for you, so you take the responsibility." He began to set the alarm and to practice each day without our hassle. Some days we feel he isn't working hard enough, but that isn't the point. The point is he has to satisfy himself, and we are now in a position to enjoy his progress without being after him all the time.

Standards are internalized when young people are asked to think about how they would like things to be. Too often young people only react to what their parents tell them to do, rather than being helped to decide what they would like to do for themselves.

A Word to the Discouraged

The Bible is a wonderful book that shows how much God understands us as people. Living is difficult and we often become discouraged when things do not seem to be going the way we would like. *"Let us not become weary in doing good,"* Paul urges us, *"for at the proper time we will reap a harvest if we do not give up"* (Galatians 6:9).

As a parent you may think your child is progressing too slowly in the area of responsibility, or maybe you feel he is not progressing at all. Don't give up! Continue to work with him. Utilize some of the suggestions presented here to see if they will work for you. We have been greatly encouraged at times to realize that parents are often the last people to know the good things that are happening in the lives of their children. Others probably see your teenager as being more responsible than you do. Give yourself a break and focus on the positive for a minute or two. This will help you to keep on keeping on!

Footnotes

[1] Paul A. Hauck, *How to Do What You Want to Do: The Art of Self Discipline* (Philadelphia: Westminster Press, 1976), p. 50.

[2] Antione de Saint-Exupery, *The Little Prince* (New York: Harcourt, Brace and Co., 1943), p. 67.

[3] Rudolf Dreikurs and Loren Grey, *A New Approach to Discipline: Logical Consequences* (New York: Hawthorne Books, Inc., 1968). p. 172.

Chapter 12

Developing Friendships Which Will Last for a Lifetime

God, you know I need this child.
Help us to be friends.

Within the Christian community there seems to be an unspoken controversy about the type of relationships parents should have with their children. I say the controversy is unspoken because it is rarely aired. People have their opinions and even make insinuations about those who relate differently to their children, but the issues are never discussed. Let's be direct. Should parents be friends with their children? Those who say "No" argue for maintaining authority and control. One father said, "If you get too close to your children, they will walk right over you." A pediatrician I once consulted for held this point of view. He said, "Don't ever admit a mistake to a child. It will cause them to lose respect for you." This negative point of view assumes that "familiarity breeds contempt." If you get too close to your children, they will not respect you and they will take you for granted.

The point of view for friendship takes the opposite approach. Those who seek to form strong friendships with their children believe that such close relationships actually produce greater respect and increase the authority of the parents with the child. Those who believe in strong parent-child friendships also point out that these friendships provide the basis for educating and training the child in values and spiritual matters.

In determining what type of relationship you should have with your teenager, one idea is very important to consider: Sound relationships, whether between husband and wife or parent and teenager, must be based upon mutual respect. This respect frees the adolescent to honor the parents, and frees the parent to be submissive to the child so that the child is not provoked to wrath. This mutual submission (discussed in Ephesians 6) is the background for solid lifelong relationships between parents and their children. Without respect there cannot be healthy love, and without love there can not be friendship.

This friendship is much more than being chums with your teenager. You are not being pals or pacifying your teenager in order to avoid trouble. Rather, this friendship is in-depth knowing, caring, and respecting; it is a closeness based on reality, not facade. True friends play together, work together, think together, feel together, solve problems together, share dreams together, and interact with God together. If you want to understand a person's needs in friendship, spend time with children who are eight to twelve years old. Notice the needs they express. Notice how giving they are. They share feelings, they ask questions, they touch, they tell you their problems, they talk about "when I grow up," they ask about God, they laugh, they cry, they help. As a parent, I find no greater joy than realizing that my children want me as their friend. I am challenged to rearrange my priorities when I realize that my busy life is often seen as rejection.

The Meaning of Friendship

So far we have approached the topic of friendship as though we automatically know what is meant. But what is friendship? Webster's dictionary defines a "friend" as "one attached to another by esteem, respect and affection . . . an intimate."[1] Based on this definition, do I have friendships within my family? Am I a friend with my spouse? Am I a friend of my teenager?

Friendship Means Being Attached

Let's look at this definition more closely. First, what does it mean to be *attached?* To be attached is to have a bond or tie with a person, to be on the same wavelength. Obviously, you can live in the same house and not be attached. The first step in developing friendships is to hook up with the other person. With tears in his eyes, a sixteen-year-boy said, "My parents don't even know I exist. We live in the same house, but in two different worlds." The desire to be attached is one of the great desires of the young human heart. As parents, we have the opportunity to take advantage of this desire. If you reach out to connect with your teenagers, sooner or later you will find them reaching back to you. If bitterness or problems have damaged your desire to reach out to them, or their desire to reach back to you, seek some professional help. It will cost you something, but remember that relationships are more important than gold. The value of a restored relationship is difficult to calculate.

Friends Are Attached by Esteem

The basis for the attachment, according to the definition of friendship, is threefold: esteem, respect, and affection. To *esteem* someone is to give them value equal to or above the value you ascribe to yourself. In theory this seems easy, but in practice it is difficult. Many parents and teenagers get into a power struggle and personal esteem is judged by whether you win or lose the battle.

Janet, age fifteen, believes that she should be able to date as she wishes. Her parents feel that she is too young and have told her she must wait until she is sixteen. The battle over dating becomes the focal point of the relationship and neither side is going to give an inch. Mom and Dad seem to forget how dependable Janet has been in the past. This, and many of Janet's other qualities, seem to vanish from the parents' minds. Esteem for Janet is lost as the parents focus on the struggle.

At the same time something is happening to Janet's view of her parents. She doesn't understand why they have changed. They used to be so understanding and loving. Now she isn't even sure she likes them. Esteem is lost and the possibilities for productive friendship are dim.

If you observe this process occurring in your family, confront the issue and try to discuss it with your teenager. Treating the issue openly and honestly will help you salvage a deteriorating situation. In power struggles no one wins. But esteem is a direct result of emphasizing the positive. The supreme challenge in esteeming others is given in Philippians 2:3-5: *"Do nothing out of selfish ambition or vain conceit, but in humility consider others better than yourselves. Each of you should look not only to your own interests, but also to the interests of others. Your attitude should be the same as that of Christ Jesus."*

Have you ever stopped to think that when you tear down your teenager, you are actually tearing yourself down? As my son once said, "You burned me, Dad, but you burned yourself worse."

Friendships Are Based on Respect

The importance of *respect* was emphasized earlier, but is worthy of a second look. What are the elements of mutual respect? Number one is a recognition of the rights of the other person. A child has rights. Those rights are no less valid than the rights of the parents. Let's consider one right that both parents and teenagers have which is often violated. This is the right to finish a task which has been started.

Billy, age thirteen, goes to his room to play his new computer game, for example. He is trying to break his record score. Just as he is getting close his mother calls him to dinner. When he doesn't respond right away she becomes angry. Mother storms down to Bill's room to confront his tardiness, and in the confusion Billy loses his concentration and fails to break his record. Both people are angry and both feel that their rights have been violated. If this conflict is not dealt with, a wedge between Billy and his parents will be created. At this point each person feels his rights have been violated and there is little mutual respect.

There are three steps for restoring mutual respect in a situation like this. First, each person should state what he wants. In this case, Billy wants to be able to play his computer game without being interrupted; Mother wants to be able to serve dinner hot and on time.

Second, each person needs to acknowledge the rights of the other, and to make a commitment to help the other person reach his goals. Mother needs to be able to say, "If you let me know when you are going for the record, I'll try not to interrupt you." Billy needs to say, "I'll try not to start a serious game when I know you almost have dinner ready." These simple statements foster an atmosphere of cooperation and respect, rather than competition and selfishness.

Third, each person needs to be willing to negotiate and give in for the sake of the other person. Billy shows respect for Mother by putting her needs above his, and Mother also shows respect for Billy's needs by allowing him to be late on those special occasions when he feels like he is going to win, even though he wasn't serious about the game when he started. The key to success is give and take. If Billy demands his way all the time something is wrong.

Parents often make the mistake of thinking their needs are more important than the needs of their adolescent. A warm dinner seems more important to a parent than a computer game victory, but in the heat of the battle, the situation is not that way in the mind of the teenager who doesn't mind cold hamburgers. Respect says, "You have the right to be who you are and I want to cooperate with you." Mutual respect is based on the premise that both persons have rights and that each person should strive to meet the needs of the other person.

Friends Share Affection

The third component of our definition of friendship is *affection.* Being friends with a stone is difficult and so is being friends with a piranha. A stone is cold and lifeless and a piranha is vicious. God has made us with a strong desire for affection. God Himself desires our affection. I love the picture of Jesus with His arms affectionately stretched out toward the people of Jerusalem, lamenting: " *'O Jerusalem, Jerusalem, you who kill the prophets and stone those sent to you, how often I have longed to gather your children together, as a hen gathers her chicks under her wings, but you were not willing'* " (Matthew 23:37). If you want to evaluate the ways you express affection toward your adolescents, take a look at your nonverbal signs. How often do you express affection or willingness to be affectionate by outstretched arms or palms open and upward? Lack of affection, on the other hand, is often shown by folded arms or lack of a smile. I have been challenged to evaluate my own level of affection by reading Ephesians 4:32: *"Be kind and compassionate to one another, forgiving each other, just as in Christ God forgave you."* The word *"kind"* means to have regard for the fragility of human personality. Being *"compassionate"* refers to furnishing the needs of the other person.

When one of our daughters was little, she enjoyed using the words "love" and "like." Maybe she was trying to learn the difference between the two. Often she would say, "Daddy, I love and I like you." I would respond by saying, "I love you and I like you, too. Give me a hug." My prayer has been that this open affection (with esteem and mutual respect) will serve as a basis for friendship as she reaches adolescence.

When people are afraid to express affection, it's sad. True, we are vulnerable when we say, "I like you and I love you." The other person may not respond with open arms. But it is also true that without expression of affection, meaningful relationships will not be formed. I have enjoyed seeing the bumper sticker which asks the provocative question, "Have you hugged your kids today?" Regardless of the poor choice of the word "kids," the message is powerful. Show affection to your children. They deserve it and so do you.

A Friend Is an Intimate

The last part of Webster's definition is just two words, *"an intimate."* To be intimate with someone, you must go beyond superficiality and be willing to really know and understand the person. As parents, we are often afraid to get to know our teenager because we are afraid we may not like the person we get to know, and then we will feel that we have failed. This trap is caused by our failure to meet our adolescent person-to-person.

Not too long ago our daughter came into our room to talk about her day. She stayed longer than expected. In fact her dad began to nod. She laughed and said, "Sure, Dad, just go to sleep. I'm not important. I'm only your daughter." She twisted my toe and smiled as she left the room. Almost simultaneously, Sandy and I turned to each other and said, "Isn't she a neat person?"

If you want to be emotionally intimate with your adolescent, you must be willing to listen. They need to tell you who they are but they can't just blurt it out. Your willingness to listen will communicate esteem, respect, and affection. Listen! You'll be glad you did.

Develop Sound Friendships

In their book, *The Heart of Friendship,* James and Savary list a number of qualities of friendship. These qualities are essential if sound friendships are to be developed.

1. Being Available to Your Teen

The first of these qualities is availability. Developing a friendship with your teenager is impossible without being available to him. Family ties are not enough to insure friendship. There must be availability. Friends spend time together.

I have often heard parents say, "I'm looking for a quality relationship with my teenager. It is quality, not quantity, that really makes the difference." This is a self-deceiving statement. At best, it's half true. You cannot have quality relationships without quantity. Just as the momentum in an athletic contest is maintained by consistent steady play, the momentum in friendships is maintained by a consistent quantity of time spent with your adolescent. I am not against quality. I believe you need to look closely at the time you do spend with your teenager to be sure that the time is spent in high quality interaction. In general, passive time (like time together in front of the television) is not as high quality as active time (such as walking and talking or playing games). When I read statistics which reveal that the average parent spends less than one minute per day talking to an individual child, I am convinced that we have kidded ourselves into thinking that a minute is quality time. Young people are not geared that way and neither are parents.

But what about the availability of the teenager? Parents often report that they want to spend time with their teenager, but the schedule of the teenager is such that he has no time for the parent. This is indeed a problem to many, but not an insurmountable one. We have found several ways of dealing with the situation. First, don't chide him for not having any time for you. He will not be able to recognize that he has any control over the situation, and you will only create a conflict.

Second, take the initiative by inviting him to do something that you know he likes to do. Shopping for a new pair of jeans, going to a ball game, or listening to a record are places to start. Think how shocked your adolescent would be if you asked him to help you pick out an album or two for the holiday season. Listen to the reasons he likes certain types of music and not others.

Third, study your teenager's daily calendar to discover the slow times in his schedule. Be available during these times. Even when he is secluded in his room, he will welcome you if you bring a pleasant disposition, a warm smile, and maybe even a little hot chocolate, cookies and milk, or soda. He may wonder what you are up to, but you will get his attention. One crucial time to be available, if possible, is right after school. This is a time when your teenager wants to talk. Be there to listen. Enjoy yourself as you hear all the latest details. I am not opposed to mothers or fathers working, but I do feel that if at all possible, one of the parents should be home when the children get home from school. The communication that will result is invaluable.

Fourth, another entry into the world of our adolescents has come through the dating process. My seventeen-year-old daughter was shocked when I asked her out to dinner. She was even more shocked when I allowed her to pick the place and suggested a couple of nice restaurants as examples. Even though she couldn't figure out why I was taking her out, we had a delightful time talking about college, boyfriends, and other aspects of growing up. My money was well spent.

If your child seems unavailable, don't be discouraged. Pursue him with love and sensitivity. He will make it difficult for you, but don't give up. The fact that you care enough to keep trying will speak volumes to him. Teenagers say they don't have time for stuffy, old parents, but secretly they desire the opportunity to be close.

2. Doing Things Together
The second important quality needed to develop a close friendship

with your teenager is doing things together. This activity flows naturally from availability. Finding an activity which both you and your teenager enjoy is sometimes difficult. Many parents give up before they get beyond this point. Recently I spent a Saturday at home with my thirteen-year-old son, Mike. We talked a little—some serious talk and some light talk. Each time I asked him if he wanted to do something with me, he turned me down. I was beginning to wonder if I was diseased. I kept my cool and we did have a good time together, watching a little of the football game, eating lunch, and playing doctor for our dog. He was probably satisfied and, by dinner time, so was I. The middle of the day was more tense because, even though I knew better, I still had an expectation that he would be more enthusiastic about some of the activities I suggested. I started to be pushy instead of being available.

One of the difficulties in doing things with your teenager is the difference in skill level. If you parents are good at tennis or racquetball, teach your teenager how to play. But if you do, remember that you are not competing for the North American Championship. Don't be condescending by playing poorly, but also avoid setting up an atmosphere of competition before the learner is ready. Be an encourager as you see his skills developing.

At other times the roles will reverse and your teenager will clearly have the skill advantage. Video games or foosball are good examples. Don't hesitate to play, but don't be surprised if you get ridiculed when you lose. Learning to win graciously is not a lesson teenagers learn easily. The teenager's ego often thrives on criticizing others, and you will not escape if you get involved. Turn a negative situation into something more positive by reminding your son or daughter to go easy on you since you have a weak ego. Remember that even though your teenager's mannerisms may be crude or rude, those mannerisms should not be taken as a personal attack. Keep the situation light and you will show him a better way. He will love it if you ask him for helpful tips and some coaching.

If possible, take turns picking activities to do together. This will help each of you to expand your skills and will also spread around the anxiety associated with doing a new activity. Each of us has a safe pad, a place where we feel most comfortable. If you want to be close to your teenager, you have to be willing to leave your safe pad at times and go to his secure place. If your teenager is comfortable on skates, you need to take the risk of going skating. Ask him first how he would feel about it. If your skating is too bad, go to a neighboring town so that neither of you will be embarrassed.

When you discover your teenager's interests, capitalize on them. If your daughter likes to hike, sew, shop, or go fishing, set aside time to do that with her. Make it an occasion. Build some anticipation. Let yourself become enthused. My oldest son is interested in hunting. We have enjoyed some special times together as I have involved myself with him and have made this something we do together. I let him be the expert, because he is, and he lets me into his world in various ways.

Often parents rely on organizations to provide the structure for doing things together. I have nothing against scouting, organized sports, or church activities, but they often provide opportunities for parents and teenagers to be together without actually doing anything together. Parents often spend more time with the other parents than they do with the teenagers themselves. The emphasis needs to be kept where it belongs—on parent-teen interaction.

3. Developing Care and Concern

A third important quality of friendship is care and concern. Webster's Dictionary defines "care" as "painstaking or watchful attention."[2] It requires commitment based on a sense of responsibility for the other person. Caring requires that you get to know your teenager's needs. Caring is not caring unless it matches up with these needs.

Too often we make the mistake of thinking that we are showing care and concern for our teenagers when we are only trying to take care of our own needs. This is illustrated by one of my first experiences in formal counseling, which was with a young man who was sixteen years old. David had a measured I.Q. of over 150, achievement test scores all above the 90th percentile, and he was flunking all of his classes at school. David was crying out for care and concern from his parents and was not getting it. He said, "Do you know how my mom tries to show love to me? She waits until I leave the house to go to school and then yells, 'David, you forgot to brush your teeth.' She doesn't really care about me at all. She just wants all those old biddies she is trying to impress to think she is a good mother. I'm sick of it."

David needed his parents to pull alongside and to hear the struggles he was facing. He was supposed to be bright and successful and no one understood what a burden that was at times. He needed someone to hear how difficult it is to be smarter than your teachers. He needed someone to hear that it isn't easy to make friends when the other young people are afraid of your brilliance. He needed someone to hear that it is discouraging to see the athletes getting all the attention while your own accomplishments go unnoticed. You cannot care for another until you take the time to focus on his needs instead of your own.

What does it mean to say "I care" to your teenager? "I care" means *I hear where you are hurting. I may not be able to fix it for you, but I will stay close to you as you try to work it out.* "I care" means *I want to help bear your burden. I want to understand so that I can help if there is a way.*

"I care" means *I want to help you to be all you can be. You have to decide what that is. I care too much to try to force you into my mold, but I also care too much to let you ignore your own goals and aspirations. I will call you to be who God has gifted you to be.* "I care" means *I want to show you how special you are to me. You are more important than what you do. I will watch you grow and become more competent in what you do, but I will not allow myself to see you only as your accomplishments.*

Finally, "I care" means *I want to love you in the way that you best receive love.* As a parent, I am aware of my tendency to want to love my children my way rather than to say, "I love you" in the language they hear. John Powell describes the process of effectively loving someone else. "Obviously the commitment to love will involve me in much careful and active listening. I truly want to be whatever you need me to be, to do whatever you need done, and I want to say whatever will promote your happiness, security, and well-being. To discover your needs, I must be attentive, caring, and open both to what you say and to what you cannot say."[3]

One of the greatest ways to show love to your teenager is to treat him with respect as a person, and allow him to grow up in a supportive environment where he feels separate but also very much a part. This type of love helps an adolescent to become autonomous.

Care and concern are sometimes best expressed by silent, prayerful vigilance. At other times care and concern require active involvement as you step forward to meet needs which are expressed. Don't be afraid to ask your adolescent to tell you which is needed, for you both know you can't read minds. Caring begins by asking and hearing.

4. Practicing Honesty

A fourth quality of friendship is honesty. Honesty is the glue which holds people together. Without honesty, relationships are either superficial and die, or they are distant and never have a chance to grow. Paul Welter has observed: "Someone has called this the stereo generation—we speak out of both sides of our mouth at the same time. However, most people who give bent messages probably don't intend to lie, or even to slant the truth. Rather, as we noticed earlier, a message is bent because it is wrapped around an unspoken, real message. One thinks one thing and says something else."[4] Many adolescents today are capable of straight talk. They want to be upfront. This will be difficult for you as a parent if you are used to relating in a less straightforward manner. The phrase, "Tell it like it is," is popular today because many recognize the need for honesty.

Lying by Omission

Dishonesty creeps into parent-teen relationships in two distinct ways. The most common is lying by omission. If you believe that what your teenager doesn't know won't hurt, you probably lie by omission. What people don't know does hurt them. It denies them the opportunity to make decisions and form opinions based upon a full awareness of the situation. It also denies them the opportunity to grapple with living and growing up in the real world.

As a parent, I would be appalled if I learned all the things that were going on with my teenagers from someone else. They, too, are upset when you fail to let them know what is going on in your life. One young person said, "I can handle some pretty tough stuff from my parents, but I can't stand it when they treat me like a child and don't tell me anything. Don't they know I have eyes and ears? I can tell something is going on."

Occasionally Sandy and I will gather the children around us to let them know what we are planning for the future. We talk about future events and activities. We talk about finances and difficulties. We talk about the things for which we are trusting God. Our children like it, especially the older ones. After one session our oldest son Mark said, "It's about time they told me something. Usually I'm the last to know."

We become upset when our children do not admit when they have done wrong or when they withhold things from us. As parents, we need to teach by example. One of the most difficult, and yet probably most valuable, things you can do with your teenager is to be honest enough to admit your shortcomings, and to take the risk of telling the whole truth.

Lying by Commission

Deliberate distortion of the truth is common in parent-teen relationships. This is lying by commission. One eighteen-year-old college freshman said, "My parents and I never tell each other the truth, not even when it wouldn't hurt anything. I come home drunk and I know Dad knows I'm drunk. Even then when he asks, I tell him I haven't been drinking. We don't know how to live without living a lie." Hopefully, not many of those who read this book will have experienced dishonesty in parent-teen relationships at this level. The warning, however, still stands. Friendship cannot be built without the basic core of honesty. Telling people what they want to hear, rather than the truth, breeds contempt, not friendship.

If honesty has not been a part of your relationship with your adolescent, sit down and own up to your past dishonesty. From that point begin to be more honest and open. Honesty sometimes hurts, but it also heals. You don't have to be brutal to be honest.

Reasons We Lie

I believe it is helpful to begin developing honesty in relationships with the belief that parents and teenagers want to be honest. The comfort level in the relationship is usually highest when honesty is highest. People usually lie, however, for one of four basic reasons: (1) fear of being hurt, (2) fear of hurting others, (3) fear of not getting their way, (4) failure to learn that honesty works. Our honesty level is affected by these four factors.

Lying to Protect Ourselves

It is true that if you tell the truth you will suffer the consequences. One mother said, "If I tell her the truth (about reading the diary), she will hate me forever." What the mother failed to realize was that as long as she was living a lie, the relationship with the daughter was slowly dying anyway. A fresh beginning was in order. Truth hurts, but lies hurt more. Truth brings things out into the open, but lies are like poison seeping into the innermost parts.

Lying to Protect Others

When lies are told to protect others, there is usually not a closeness in the relationship. Although Ephesians 4:15 refers primarily to communicating sound doctrine, it is also applicable to communicating other information as well: *"Instead, speaking the truth in love, we will in all things grow up into him who is the Head, that is, Christ."* Withholding the truth, even if it is for the sake of protecting others from hurt, is a form of manipulation. Withholding the truth prevents closeness. The truth may hurt but it is the truth. If you develop the type of relationship with your teenager where truth thrives, you have the basis for a lifetime friendship. John White has pointed out that parents and teenagers must teach each other how to tell the truth. Because of our fallen nature, telling the truth does not come naturally. He suggests an approach for developing a more honest relationship with your teenager.

> If we're to have a good relationship we've got to trust one another. Trust has to be learned. Just now I can't trust you because you've taught me not to. I want to learn to trust you again, but it'll take time. Even when you're telling me the truth I'll be thinking of all the times you've lied to me. If I act suspicious when you're telling me the truth, it's at least partly your own fault. You've fooled me so many times, Jane, that just now it's hard for me to accept all you say. I want to believe you, but you're going to have to teach me, and that will need time.[5]

Lying to Get Our Way

Withholding the truth in order to get your way is also a form of manipulation. Many parents lie or at least shade the truth in order to move their adolescents in certain directions. At best, this is still hypocrisy. If the facts won't help us to get our way with our teens, then we probably want the wrong things. Parents often lie to their teenagers about such things as drugs and friends. The teenagers know that they have better facts than their parents and thus lose confidence in the parents. In other instances the teenagers follow the parents' direction for a while and then rebel when they realize the whole truth has not been told.

One of my colleagues who works with teenagers that are on drugs often starts by giving each teen a test about drugs. Teenagers usually have more facts than their parents. My colleague gains teenagers' confidence by acknowledging the facts that they do have. This gives him the base from which to confront them about their errors. He might say something like, "Well, Bill, you got 95%. That's pretty good. You did make one error, however, that could cost you your life. PCP, angel dust, is much more dangerous than you realize. Here is a short article to read." The point I am making is this: Distortion of the truth in order to manipulate or to get your way usually backfires. It destroys friendships rather than making them meaningful.

Learning to Practice Honesty

A teenaged client stated, "I never knew I could tell my parents the truth. I'm not sure I even know how." Some parents have echoed the same sentiment. In all cases my advice has been the same. Take the risk of being honest in some ways that you have not been honest before. God will give you creative solutions to the problems which arise in your family if you ask Him. Honesty is a basic ingredient of any creative solution.

One of the ways parents should *"train a child in the way he should go"* (Proverbs 22:6) is by the honest behavior they model. If you want honesty from your adolescents, show them how. You will be overjoyed as you find a new basis for friendship.

5. Maintaining Confidentiality and Loyalty

A fifth important element of friendship is confidentiality and loyalty. If you want to be able to talk *with* your teenagers, you need to be careful not to talk *about* them. As adults, we often make the error of thinking that because they are our children, it won't matter how or to whom we talk about them.

As a parent I often feel anxious about one or more of my children. I am sometimes tempted to discuss this with others as a means of relieving my anxiety. I have learned to be cautious, because I have seen the effects of saying things publicly which were spoken to me in private. Such loose words can undermine the confidence which a teenager has in his parents. I was once told, "I have feelings, too, Dad. How do you feel when people talk about you?"

Don't assume that it is all right if you talk about certain things related to your teenagers. When in doubt, ask them. I often use anecdotes from our family life as examples when I write or speak at a conference. I do so only after I have asked my children for permission. This permission should be gained prior to the time it is needed, not during the presentation. Young people deserve the right to be able to say "No." I am not just relating my life, but I'm sharing theirs as well. They have a right to decide how "public" they want to be. I asked my youngest son for permission to relate an incident and he delighted me with his response, "I guess so, Dad. Why not, if it might help someone else?" He felt a part of my ministry. The outcome would have been much different, however, if he had heard me talk about him without being given the choice. To be loyal is to respect the rights of the other person. If you fail to offer your teenager the same loyalty you give and receive from other friends, you will not develop a lasting friendship. Be sensitive to the needs of your adolescent in these areas. Treat him with respect and you will receive respect. Teenagers are naturally loyal to their parents, especially when they have been the recipients of loyal friendships.

6. Seeking to Understand Your Teen

One final quality of friendship is understanding or empathy. This is the quality which allows friendships to deepen. One of the greatest longings of the human heart is the longing to be understood. Yet few teenagers feel understood by their parents, and few parents feel understood by their teenagers. One prominent source of this mis-understanding is the expectation that our teenagers will think as we think. If you approach your teenager expecting him to be like you, you will not understand him. On the other hand, if you forego your expectation and simply seek to discover what your teenager thinks or feels, you will begin to understand him, and this understanding will be perceived by your teenager as empathy. The following quote from David Elkind indicates why we so often misunderstand our adolescents: "One of the most serious and pernicious misunderstandings about young children is that they are most like adults in their thinking and least like us in their feelings. In fact, just the reverse is true, and children are most like us in their feelings and least like us in their thinking."[6]

In chapter 2 we pointed out that adolescents are going through a transition process from concrete to abstract thinking. This change often creates havoc for parents who are trying to understand their adolescents, because one minute your child is symbolic or abstract and the next he is totally black and white in his thinking. Rather than being frustrated by this, recognize and accept it as normal for your teenager at this point in his development. Be patient in exploring your point of view and be doubly patient in understanding the point of view of your teenager. Remember that friendships are built in understanding, not on winning arguments. Haim Ginott cites an example of the way understanding deepens the parent-teen relationship.

When Clara, age 14, criticized modern painting, Mother did not dispute her opinion. Nor did she condemn her taste.

Mother: You don't like abstract art?
Clara: I sure don't. It's ugly.
Mother: You prefer representational art?
Clara: What's that?
Mother: You like it when a house looks like a house and a tree like a tree, and a person like a person.
Clara: Yes.
Mother: Then you like representational art.
Clara: Imagine that. All my life I liked representational art and didn't know it.[7]

Understanding and empathy are similar. You cannot have empathy without understanding. To empathize is to identify with someone else, to feel what the other person is feeling. Obviously you will not empathize with everyone all the time. The key is to seek to empathize with your family members at least some of the time. Allow yourself to live mentally in your teenagers' shoes. Feel what life is like for them. Notice the pressures they experience. Don't try to fix them or their situations right now. Just try to understand them. When parents fix things for them, children do not develop the self-confidence they need as they become adults. Resisting the temptation to fix things for your teenager is difficult. It goes against parental instincts which have been operative since before the child was born. Even though it is difficult to allow your teenager to struggle, it is the most loving thing you can do. I recently heard my daughter on the telephone with a friend. The friend's emotional needs were high and she wanted my daughter to promise that she would spend more time with her. She wanted an exclusive relationship. The tension in my daughter's voice grew as she tried to help her friend realize that she could not be what the friend wanted. By the time the long conversation ended, Marcy was near tears. She came out of the room and I held my hands out to her. I listened quietly as she released her frustration. As she finished, I could tell she was struggling over whether or not she had handled it right. She was relieved and seemed reassured when I said that from what I could hear, I didn't know how she could have handled it any better. Her reply was simple, "Thanks, Dad."

Our greatest model of empathy is Jesus Christ. In Hebrews, where He is pictured as our great High Priest, we are told that He is able to sympathize with our weaknesses (see Hebrews 4:14-17). Because of this we are told to approach the throne of God with confidence. Similarly, if you are empathetic with your teenagers, they will have greater confidence to approach you. This type of relationship will be a source of joy for both of you.

Getting Started at Building Friendship

The qualities of friendship which we have discussed are all important in establishing a sound, life-long friendship with your teenager. However, for many of you, moving in the desired direction will be difficult. The following excerpt from *The Little Prince* is helpful.

"One only understands the things that one tames," said the fox to the Little Prince, who was in search of a friend.

"If you want a friend, tame me."

"What must I do, to tame you?" asked the little prince.

"You must be very patient," replied the fox.

"First you will sit down at a little distance from me—like that—in the grass. I shall look at you out of the corner of my eye, and you will say nothing. Words are the source of misunderstanding. But you will sit a little closer to me, every day."[8]

The phrase, "words are the source of misunderstandings" needs to be heeded. Many parents talk themselves out of the possibility of friendship. Remember to sit a little closer each day—not to lecture or instruct, but to hear even a whisper. Do not sit *on* the teenager. Sit *by* the teenager. If you don't know the difference, ask him. He will tell you.

Because I grew up on a farm in eastern Oregon, I learned much from my experiences with animals. As a youngster I had a wild horse that I could not catch. Before I knew better I would run frantically after him, often with tears streaming down my cheeks. I was never successful in catching him.

My father helped me learn the importance of patience. He told me that if I took a pan of oats and sat quietly in the pasture, the natural curiosity of the animal would draw him to me. At first I grew tired and left before he came. The horse learned, however, that I was associated with the pan of oats which I left. Eventually he came and ate the oats from the pan while I watched. One day he even ate from my hand. My tears of frustration were turned to tears of joy. He was my friend.

Friendships formed now with your teenagers will be invaluable to them and to you in the future. This is the payoff for your labors. This is the great opportunity of adolescence. Don't let it slip by you. As my teenagers say, "Go for it."

Footnotes

[1]*Webster's New Collegiate Dictionary,* 1977 ed., s.v. "friend."

[2]*Webster's New Collegiate Dictionary,* 1977 ed., s.v. "care."

[3]John Powell, *Unconditional Love* (Niles, Ill.: Argus Communications, 1978), p. 64.

[4]Paul Welter, *Family Problems and Predicaments: How to Respond* (Wheaton, Ill.: Tyndale House Publishers, Inc.), p. 48.

[5]John White, *Parents in Pain* (Downers Grove, Ill.: InterVarsity Press, 1979), p. 72.

[6]David Elkind, *Children and Adolescents: Interpretative Essays on Jean Piaget* (New York: Oxford Press, 1974), p. 51.

[7]Haim G. Ginott, *Between Parent and Teenager* (New York: Avon Books, 1969), p. 52.

[8]Antione de Saint-Exupery, *The Little Prince* (New York: Harcourt, Brace and Co., 1943), p. 67.

Staying in Touch, a 6-part video series with study guide based on the book *You Try Being a Teenager,* is now available either through Video Bible Library, Box 17515, Portland, OR 97217, or Wilson Communication Enterprises, 600 Avenue A, Suite 210, Lake Oswego, OR 97034.